XC

STARFISH

STARFISH

One family's tale of triumph after tragedy

by Tom Ray
with additional material
by Nic Ray

metro

Published by John Blake Publishing Ltd,
3 Bramber Court, 2 Bramber Road,
London W14 9PB, England

www.johnblakebooks.com

www.facebook.com/johnblakebooks [f]
twitter.com/jblakebooks [t]

This edition published in 2017

ISBN: 978 1 78606 512 4

British Library Cataloguing-in-Publication Data:

A catalogue record for this book is available from the British Library.

Design by www.envydesign.co.uk

Printed in Great Britain by CPI Group (UK) Ltd

1 3 5 7 9 10 8 6 4 2

Papers used by John Blake Publishing are natural, recyclable products made from wood
grown in sustainable forests. The manufacturing processes conform to the environmental
regulations of the country of origin.

Every attempt has been made to contact the relevant copyright-holders, but some were
unobtainable. If there are any queries, we would be grateful if the appropriate people
could contact us.

John Blake Publishing is an imprint of Bonnier Publishing
www.bonnierpublishing.com

To Nina.
We made it.

CONTENTS

Starfish

A sea star that has the ability to regenerate amputated limbs must first undergo a repair phase to heal the exposed wound. Once the wound is healed, the sea star can begin to generate new cells, which in turn sparks new growth. Regeneration can take anywhere from several months to years.

FOREWORD
BY JOANNE FROGGATT

I first heard Tom and Nic's story back in 2013 when I was approached by Bill Clark to play Nic in the feature film he was developing. I was overwhelmed then, and continue to be to this day, with admiration for the courage, determination and just simple love that this couple have showed each other over such a long and challenging journey together. Compared to the daily ups and downs we all face in our lives, their ups and downs have been like conquering Everest!

I can honestly say I didn't think twice about saying yes. I joined the team who were working to put the film together and have been delighted to be involved from then till now as an Executive Producer. It took a couple more long years to get the film made, and through all that time

I – and soon Tom Riley too, who had signed up to play Tom – were wondering how it would be when we actually got in a room with the real Rays themselves. I have played real people before and it always brings new challenges. In this case I knew what a personal and intimate story we were aiming to make and how delicate these things can be. In addition, I knew how enthusiastically and bravely Tom and Nic had collaborated with Bill in developing the film and wanted to make sure we did not raise their hopes that the film was about to happen while we were still trying to lock down the finance. In independent film this is never easy, and so the months passed.

And then – finally – the longed for breakthrough, and from there I am glad to say it all happened really fast and we were headed to the Rays' home county, Rutland, for the shoot. That long-postponed, long-anticipated meeting with Tom and Nic was finally about to happen.

We all met for supper at the Falcon Hotel in Rutland with director Bill and producer Pippa – two real Rays and two screen Rays. Surreal doesn't really do it justice. A bit of polite and excited chat, then thoughts of a second glass of wine, and then Tom said, 'Shall we get a bottle?' and we were off – Tom and Nic talked and talked, and it was almost as if they had always been part of us, and even us of them.

When we started filming we wanted to be sure to capture the vibrancy of the 'before' – of their relationship and their precious time with their daughter Grace before Tom's sepsis struck. Film requires – unlike the luxury of a book – the compression of real life and time, and our job is to capture the essence. I was thrilled that Tom Riley and I managed to capture something of the joy of the Rays' early time together.

Tom Ray was on set with us a lot as we worked through the filming schedule and the crisis that overwhelmed the family – sharing memories and issues with Tom Riley, and doubling for him in a couple of particularly tough scenes in which the authenticity of his amputations was always going to be more powerful than any film visual effects. Nic was often away working ahead of us with the art department – they had quickly spotted her talent as an artist and roped her into the team, creating brickwork from sheets of plywood, recreating a hospital set in an old aircraft hangar... This last location was, I knew, a difficult one for her. Tom's time in hospital was largely a blur to him as he spent much of it in a coma. For Nic, however, this period is still acutely painful to recall. She was eight months pregnant, had a three year old at home, and life as she and her beloved husband knew it had changed overnight and forever. As we recreated Nic's first visits to Tom in intensive care I knew that, as I worked to get into her head, she was quietly taking herself away into a different zone, far from the relentless hustle and bustle of a film set.

A year later and our film has come out to a lovely response. I know the whole film team is delighted that we have been able to do our bit to raise awareness of the devastation that sepsis can cause, and this whole campaign continues to be very close to my heart. There is so much that can be done to improve survival rates and outcomes for those survivors. This is not about complex and expensive medical research, it is much more simply about being aware, and as the UK Sepsis Trust tell us – 'Just ask, could it be sepsis?'

I am delighted now that Tom and Nic have these pages in which to share their journey directly. They have been so generous in letting others into their hearts and minds, and it is wonderful to be able to read their own account unbrokered by the creative process of film making.

I hope the two endeavours can stand as fitting witness to an extraordinary couple. Theirs is a journey on which I have been honoured and privileged to play my small part and the continuing journey that Tom and Nic are now on is one of such great positivity. That's the power of love. That simple.

With my love to you both
Jo

INTRODUCTION

We live with our two young children, Grace and Frederic.

On 9 December 1999 at around 6pm Tom took a short nap and started to feel fuzzy headed and headachy. He went to bed around 10.30pm that night.

He woke at 3 o'clock in the morning the next day as he was feeling nauseous. He went to sleep in the second bedroom as he did not want to wake me up. But he did. Between 3am and 10am he was sick several times and was also complaining of violent headaches, stomach ache and dehydration.

Late mid-morning I rang our GP for advice. He prescribed domperidone as he thought that Tom might have food poisoning and said to call back if things worsened. At lunchtime Tom took the domperidone but he brought it up immediately. The sickness eased. He took a second dose. He stayed in bed to sleep as he still had strong headaches. He was also complaining of feeling cold and sensitive to light. I noted he did not have a temperature, and he seemed distant.

At around 6 o'clock that evening Tom was severely dehydrated and asked me to go out for Lucozade. He said that his feet were feeling cold and at 6.30pm he called me on my mobile to ask me to come home quickly as he was feeling very poorly. When I returned home I found Tom semi-conscious and I immediately contacted the on-call doctor who advised me to call an ambulance immediately. I asked if Tom might be having a reaction to the domperidone and the doctor said that this was a possibility.

At 7.30pm Tom was taken by ambulance to Peterborough District Hospital Accident and Emergency. He was admitted by a student nurse, we described his symptoms and we told the nurses that his feet and hands were freezing and numb. Tom was given intravenous fluids and was also given sweetened orange juice as we were told that his blood sugar levels were unusual. At this stage, the doctor looking after Tom was wondering whether he had diabetes and a chest X-ray was taken as his breathing was shallow.

The rash that was likened to pin pricks on admission was beginning to spread over Tom's chest and face and the student nurse informed us that Tom would be admitted to a medical ward for observation overnight but there might be a delay. Tom remained in the A&E department until very late into the evening, during which time his symptoms continued. The rash across his face was developing very quickly as was the complete loss of sensation to his extremities, such as his hands and feet.

The student nurse accompanied Tom to the medical ward and on the way he passed the doctor as he was going off duty. Tom and the nurse emphasized to the doctor that the loss of sensation to his extremities was worsening and the doctor said that he was going off duty but that another doctor, P, knew everything.

Over the next few hours his condition deteriorated dramatically. Tom's blood pressure was dropping and the rash was turning to a purple colouring all over his body and face and there was also considerable swelling. His eyes were weeping blood. He had diarrhoea and vomited violently. He was very distressed. Nursing staff were having difficulty with blood pressure monitoring. There were large numbers of patients on the ward and the nurses seemed unable to monitor as appropriate. To my knowledge, he was not seen by a medical consultant, though I believe the Medical Registrar may have spoken to a consultant by phone in A&E.

Tom was eventually admitted to ITU in the early hours of the morning. At this point the staff nurse said that she believed Tom should have been admitted to ITU four hours earlier. Tom had total organ failure by this point. I was informed that he had a 1 in 10 chance of survival, although treatment for pneumococcal septicaemia had now begun.

The diagnosis had now been made but due to the advanced stage of the disease he had to undergo numerous amputations. Both his hands were amputated below the elbow and both his feet were cut off below the ankle. His lips and nose and the lower half of his face were amputated. He then had to undergo further amputation surgery to amputate both his legs to the mid-calf. His spleen was found to have been destroyed and his adrenal function was severely impaired. Tom is consequently taking prophylactic penicillin and hydrocortisone in perpetuity.

On 2 February 2000, Tom was transferred to the plastic surgery ward at Addenbrooke's Hospital for continued plastic surgery. He was subsequently transferred to a rehabilitation unit. He finally left hospital on 8 August 2000, eight months after admission. He has had numerous operations since for facial reconstruction. This will continue indefinitely.

Prior to his admission to hospital, Tom and I ran our own conference/video production business but following his illness neither of us has been able to work. I was also 8 and a half months pregnant at the time of Tom's illness with our second child, which brought additional financial pressures. During this time we relied on benefits. Our previous partnership was dissolved in August 2001 and I now work as a sole trader, on a much reduced basis.

9 December 1999

One moment I'm at home, sitting on the sofa watching TV; next, I am slowly sliding to the floor – my hands and face are turning black, my body shaking. I want Lucozade but Nic grabs the phone instead. Forty-five minutes later we're in an ambulance, tearing down the A1 towards Peterborough. I'm flat on my back, dipping in and out of consciousness, feeling like I'm going to die.

Sepsis strikes up like a fire in the forest, kills quickly, switching off the lights of life in hours, tearing limb from limb, leaving a shaking and humiliated half of you alive to grin and bear it like a wounded animal. It tried to kill me that night, and it had huge help from the staff at Peterborough hospital, who really didn't seem to have a clue. Feet, hands, gone. Legs below the knee, gone. Mouth, nose, twisted, scarred and swollen. Fate, rolling over and twisting simply.

January 2000

Across the hospital concourse, in the early hours, our son Freddy is born.

February 2000

I wake from eleven weeks in a coma and there's just two-thirds of me left. I wake repeatedly, for just a few minutes at a time, alone in a white hospital room. There are so many thick plastic tubes coming in and going out of me, I cannot move. My head is wrapped in bandages, with only slits for my eyes. A steel spring mechanism, something like an animal trap, or restraint, keeps my mouth permanently open, my teeth bared. My heart is wired to a monitor that bleeps intermittently.

Light comes and goes at the window. I have no idea who or where I am.

It takes a few days for me to work it out, but it seems to me that there is something terribly wrong with my body. Something that's not normal for a human, and something I really don't like. Even though I can hardly move, I sense it. *The shape my arms and legs make under the hospital bed blankets is nightmarishly curtailed.* My face feels ripped red and raw, as if somebody has poured molten acid on it, and as if it has cooked.

I close my eyes, hoping it's all a nightmare. During the bright white noise and commotion of the day, I try to screw my eyes shut tightly and pretend to be asleep. When

I open them a millimetre, I become aware of the shapes
of visitors who come to sit beside me. Some of them have
words, others bring only their silence and sadness.

There are doctors who come to stare at me, because
they say I am a medical miracle: a man that survived a
psychopathic killer of a disease that until now has spared
no-one. And come they do, in numbers, to stand and
stare and marvel at the havoc sepsis can wreak on the
human body, tearing it to shreds in the space of hours,
stripping and splitting the soul.

I am like the cold dead body of one of Christ's disciples,
left to hang for people to gawp at. I am wrecked, torn,
splayed and stuck like a pig. I am fed liquid meals through
a tube into my stomach. Every now and then, as the drugs
wax and wane like an evil moon in my bloodstream, my
soul flies, then crashes.

There is a voice that whispers to me on the pillow. I
have no idea if it is part of the dream, a hallucination, or
reality. I feel only that I can cling to it – to the quality
of its kindness, to its warmth, to its humanity. It seems
to say, *sleep now – everything is over, everything is done.* It
talks of children, bringing news of a girl called Grace
who loves me very much (although I don't know why or
how that can be) and a new baby boy called Freddy, who
apparently needs me to get better. It is a voice like warm
water sprinkled on my eyelids, soft and kind and gentle.
It stirs a part of me, even in my coma, reminding me

that I'm thirty-eight and in love with the most beautiful woman in the world. It tells me that one third of me is gone but what's left is enough; that the thing is, above all, to survive.

HAMBLETON,
2005

Winter morning, early. Big blue sky, patched here and there with whispers of white. I don't stop to have breakfast, I just get in the car and drive. Out of Oakham, past the new housing estate, and turning right onto the peninsula road. I follow it for two miles, straight, with Rutland Water spreading out sheer, silver, splendid on either side, then veering to the right as the road winds up the steep hill into the village. Past The Finches pub on the left, at the top, as I emerge onto the only crossroads. Ketton Road forging on through the village, millionaire houses on both flanks, then blindly into another couple of miles of farmland. After that, I know that the tarmac just dips down there into the lake, disappearing into Rutland Water.

I know it leads nowhere.

And so I stop in the centre of the village, by the churchyard. The trees by the black wrought-iron churchyard gate are a hundred feet tall; they tower over me. Shafts and spindles of December sunlight shoot through, playing out shapes and shadows on the road.

This is the place where I felt happiest of all in my entire life. But now I am locked out. Excluded. I'm just a visitor from the past, mocked by a cacophony of rooks.

Nobody else is around.

Here is peace; here is isolation. No traffic, aeroplanes, footsteps or chatter. No TV news, emails or distractions of any kind. Hambleton is another world, a place removed. I am surrounded by the largest inland lake in Britain, cleansed by it. Across the road, No. 2 Post Office Cottages is just how I left it, four years ago.

I had wanted to sit here and write a detailed description of the building as it appears to me, but the laptop I've brought has been password protected and I'm not on the list. It's been hard enough to drive here, with my artificial arms and legs, and to lift the computer from the passenger seat. Now the bone at the lower end of my right amputated arm is painful, bruised, and sore. With my electronic prosthetic hand, I scramble to pick up a tiny pink mobile phone and prod at the minuscule buttons in a vain attempt to phone home for the password. After ten full minutes, and four attempts, I give up.

That's what things are like these days. So instead I just listen to the birdsong.

My false legs feel heavy and awkward, tucked into the well in front of the driving seat. My memories are vigorous, fluid and strong, but I cannot stretch my body without causing pain and regretting it instantly.

What am I looking for? Understanding. A sense that there are reasons for the things that have happened in my life. Not necessarily justification. Part of growing up is learning that some key things in our lives are fundamentally beyond our control. We know that so much of life is random, and will always keep changing – but will we always be losing the things that we love most of all? Is there a way we can stop that from happening in our lives?

Post Office Cottages is one long, high building right at the entrance to the village. It's divided now into three houses, each built in substantial honey-coloured stone, and every brick is nearly a full foot wide. The arched doorways to the cottages are in heavy, monastic, dark brown oak; the windows are mullioned, in leaded glass, and the front of the building is largely covered in ivy.

The cottages at either end of the building have tall first-floor windows, but No. 2, in the middle, has just a smaller gabled outlook, from the main bedroom – where Nic and I used to sleep, with little Grace in her cot, in the corner. The roof is long, wide and low, covered right across in ancient moss. There are huge stone chimneys at either end.

I once tried to clean the moss from that roof – before my feet and hands were cut from me. I thought it was unsightly, so I got a ladder and long brush, and I went up there to try and scrape it off. It was typical of me, taking on a huge pointless task to try and make things better. But it made no difference, and the moss has grown back now, just as I knew it would.

The cottage at the right-hand side was the old Postal & Telegraph Office. It has a beautiful clock on its lower wall, and intricate Art Deco signage on its massive oak front door. When we lived at No. 2, the old Postmaster was still resident. The Post Office itself had closed long ago, and Bill had become a lonely widower, who looked after himself and tended the house and gardens well into his nineties.

He used to run that Post Office with his wife and no doubt they had many happy years there, but Hambleton village had been stranded by the flooding of Rutland Water in 1972, and his whole existence changed completely. His wife died, the Post Office closed and he retired; everything had gone. Except it hadn't. He once invited me in there, into what should have been his front lounge, and yet there it still was, laid out before me, an entire post World War I telegraph office, complete with counters, advertising posters, letter racks and a wooden sign on a chain that said 'Please Queue Here'.

On the other side of the building, at No. 4, was a holiday cottage, used only infrequently.

Nic and I lived at No. 2 from 1996 to 2001. I'd come from London and Nic had moved from Leicester, to one of the quietest places you could wish for, a fairy-tale village in the middle of a huge lake. The sound of the birds filled our days, and at night the wind rapped at the casement windows blowing like black chaos through the trees in the churchyard. It was enchanting.

And here I am, nine years later, after so much damage has been done. I'm trying to find my way back into the house, to step through the door in my mind, and to get back home.

Through the wide, heavy black wrought iron gate, along the gravel path there is a long low grey stone wall along the right-hand side, a foot thick. On the left is the front garden, and in the middle the magnolia tree we planted in 1997 when Grace was born. It's twelve feet high now, and it's gone a little bit out of control.

As I approach the house I notice the solidity of the bricks, the thickness of the mullion around the stone windows, the enormous frame of the oak front door. There are steps up to a broad terrace, a little area to the right-hand side underneath the study window, where

I placed a post box that I'd made out of plywood. I remember, I painted it a beautiful shade of emerald green and stencilled it carefully in gold letters. I was a young father, trying to make things nice for everyone.

That box has gone now, but the bell is still there, at the door. A proper brass bell that you have to strike, with a chain, to make a ringing sound.

Inside is a tiny hallway. No, not a hall – it's just the space at the bottom of the stairs. I know there are thirteen stairs there, because when I was first back from hospital the only way I could get up them was to sit at the very bottom, get Nic to brace her forearms underneath the stumps of my legs, then use the elbows left above my amputated arms to jamb myself upwards, one step at a time. I used to count each tread of the stairs as we progressed, and pause at the top, breathless, looking down.

I remember the carpet was soft, thick, and the colour of gold. There were four rooms on the ground floor, none of them very large. The lounge was a square room, with a rather plain fireplace that we tended not to use. We put our dresser against one wall, our sofa against another, an armchair in one corner, a TV in another – and that more or less filled up the place. But there was a beautiful thick bolstered bookshelf running along the right-hand wall, and that pretty mullioned window with the leaded windows, framing the ivy climbing outside – so the view onto the garden was joyous and green. The room was dark, cosy, and a fine place to sit in on a winter's night, with a nice glass of wine and a good reason not to be venturing out into the darkness. But if you did go out at night, you saw a million stars. There were no street lights on the peninsula, so our night sky was diamond-encrusted.

The drawing room was two steps across the space at the bottom of the stairs, and exactly the same size as the lounge – square, evenly proportioned. It had the same stone mullioned windows, with the ivy hanging in them, then against the back an entire wall of books that housed all the editions Nic and I had collected along the way through our university degrees. I spent many hours at the desk in that room, working at the computer, listening to music, staring out at the road. Often I would just sit there, trying to work out how I had been so fortunate to wind up in such a special place. I was in love with life.

The kitchen is out the back – long, thin. We asked the friend of a friend to put in new wooden units, which he painted yellow, and we had thick brown carved worktops. Quarry tile floor, latch doors to the pantry and an understairs cupboard. There was another pretty leaded window out onto the cottage garden, and a huge wooden door at the back with a racing hare carved into it. That led out to a scruffy little lean-to, where we kept a dishwasher and a washer-dryer.

The only other room downstairs was the bathroom

with an old chipped iron roll-top bath, more quarry tiles, a big white washbasin, and the WC. The latch-door to the bathroom led directly off the kitchen, and there was a small window onto the garden. You could relax in the bath looking out at the leaves on the trees. Like so much else about the cottage, it was dark, a bit old-fashioned – half inconvenient, half quaint.

Between 1996 and 1999, what kind of life did we lead, out there on the peninsula?

There were times when it was difficult, when the role reversal between me and Nic grated; periods when Nic wished she could spend more time at home with our young daughter Grace, and times when my change of role from banker to house husband became too hard to handle. It took me some time to grow into it. Like the cottage itself, our lifestyle was a little rough round the edges, and a bit untidy in the corners – but somehow it worked.

After decades of living in London and the South East, the sudden transmigration to a village that time had forgotten was a source of daily fascination. We could walk down the hill from the cottage to the lake, watch the moonlight catch on the water, and feel like we had stumbled into a dream. We were very much in love with each other. I remember being upstairs, in our bedroom at the cottage, and just listening to the night wind. It was violent, huge, like an ocean. But I felt safe, behind the thick stone walls, knowing I was not alone, that my beautiful Nic was downstairs, that our bonds of love would keep us strong.

Memories shatter. Take a pane of glass down the gravel path in the back garden, past the garden seat made out of fallen branches, through the trees at the back, framing the wicker gate. Lean it up against the old pigsty and outhouse, then hit it hard with a hammer. Then you'll know what's in my head. A thousand bits of glass in amongst the grass — try to pick it up, and it will cut you.

I've taken so many tablets since I became ill, I can hardly tell you how many. I once wrote a list of them and it was like a cruel kind of poetry. When I think of myself as a young boy, how healthy and strong I was, it makes me weep inside.

I often think the tablets have made it harder for me to remember. More damaging, perhaps was the initial period of coma, when I was pumped so full of antibiotics and kept for weeks under sedation that when I finally came out of it, I didn't even know who I was. I had to ask Nic twenty times what had happened to me, and it wasn't until I registered that it couldn't be reversed that I started to cry. So forgive me if this narrative is inadequate and maudlin in places. There are areas in my brain that have been abandoned, like boarded-up pubs in seaside towns.

I drive slowly down the hill to the edge of the water. The servo motors of my myoelectric hands whirr dry and angry as I come to a halt, then reach around the steering column to switch off the ignition. I look at the cold, flat expanse of water and I realise this is where my story ends.

EASTWOOD, ESSEX, 1965–72

Truly Scrumptious

My dad is an actor – he's on TV and in the theatre. He's not a household name, but in his own terms, he's always in work, and what you'd call successful. But from very early on my mum takes great pains to let everyone know that he is a rogue and a scoundrel, a person who can never be trusted. Throughout my childhood, he is mostly absent: he has women all around town, he's always running, always broke, and always in a fix. He's always fighting with Mum in the back kitchen of our pebble-dash semi in Eastwood, Essex. I'm ten years old, kicking a football against the back wall of our house, flicking it up into the air, controlling it with my head, letting it roll down my shoulder, down my arm. I'm good – really good. I know all the tricks.

My brother Adam, twelve, is sitting in a broken garden chair reading a comic. Nina, our fourteen year old sister, is nowhere to be seen – she's probably in her room writing another fan letter to The Monkees. There's an endless Essex sky – a huge blanket of white-grey cloud that just sits above, immovable and stupid, occasionally spewing rain. From inside the house, we hear my mum shout:

'You fucking bastard!'

I trap the ball as it comes back to me, and then I pick it up. Adam lifts his head from his comic. We exchange a look; we know what's going on, what's about to happen. A door slams. Then we hear the sound of Dad's footsteps pounding down the stairs. Moments later, there's the sound of Mum following him down. Chasing him.

Adam and I go into our garage at the end of the garden. We put Procol Harum's 'A Whiter Shade of Pale' on the record player, and turn it up loud to drown out the noise. We don't have a car, we never go on holidays, and money is always tight. It is something to fight over, between my parents, on the rare occasions Mum catches up with Dad. While he's up in London, running around town with his girlfriends, she is busy trying to make ends meet.

Occasionally, she gets help from Dad's parents, who live just a couple of streets away from us, and sometimes from her own mum and dad, forty miles closer into London, in Upminster. This takes the form of a five-pound note, or a shopping bag full of tins, an occasional sheet of Green Shield Stamps. But it's hardly what you might call a permanent fix. It must make things extremely difficult for Mum, but although I'm aware that we are not by any circumstances what other people would call rich, by and large I live in blissful ignorance.

I don't think about it that much. After all I have clothes on my back and intermittently there is food on the table. There's even pocket money, and it's joyous every Saturday morning when we hold out our hands to receive it: shillings and pennies, heavy coins, rattling in the pockets of Adam's and my shorts as we run down the garden to grab our bikes. Then he and I are straight out down the back drive, on to Eastwood Rise, down the hill to the local parade of shops. With just a small amount of change we can buy plenty: a comic, a great big bag of sweets, and a chocolate bar. We gather outside the shop with our friends, comparing our treasure, and devouring it.

I come home from school one day, and Nina's gone. For some reason, she's been sent away to a boarding school in a place faraway called Dorset. There's no warning of this, it just happens, and suddenly her bedroom is empty. Adam and I go in there and we flick through her records to see which ones she's left.

Then, on another Saturday, we get a call from Dad. He has tickets for Spurs v. Chelsea, and we're to travel up to town and meet him. Adam and I are handed over at Liverpool Street station and Mum gets the chance to spend an afternoon going round the shops.

It's strange and wonderful for me and my brother to see the football stars of the day, right up close. For Chelsea, there's big Ron 'Chopper' Harris in midfield and goal scorer Peter Osgood up front, Pat Jennings is in goal for Spurs, he's looking for Jimmy Greaves up front with every long clearance. We've only ever seen them on TV, and in black and white, but suddenly we're there, at White Hart Lane, surrounded by forty thousand screaming fans. For the first time we see how adults behave, *en masse*, in a pack. It's brilliant! And frightening. But it gets worse, after the game. We have to travel back across London, on the Tube, which is in itself a disorientating experience. Adam and I are unfamiliar with the long underground tunnels and walkways, with their dim yellow lights. Adverts and notices on the walls as we pass by seem bizarre, almost from another world. The stink of cigarette smoke and the perpetual wafts of warm, stale air make us feel sick and exhausted.

By 6pm we're at the station concourse. The day is tired and almost done. It's winter, so it's dark already, and rain is sheeting down onto the glass roof, high above. There are hordes of shoppers and visitors spilling out from the underground exits and like us, they are eager to get home. The caff is still open, and I'm looking over to it, hoping I might still get a meal. Adam has gone to a vending machine by the toilets underneath the stairs to try and get an Aztec chocolate bar – but Mum hasn't let me go. She's holding on to my hand too tightly, and I'm eager to get free.

I notice that people are starting to stare, because Mum is talking very loudly. Or shouting, rather, at Dad, reaching out and pushing him. I hear my dad say: 'I will come home, I promise' and I'm thinking: *I bloody well hope he doesn't!* I hear him saying he's going to Ireland, to make a film with a man called David Hemmings, and that Adam and I can come too – for a holiday.

'I'm trying to make things right,' he tells Mum.

'You want to take the kids on holiday – with *her?* With *that woman?*'

I get my hand loose and break free. I'm getting scared now, because my mum's voice is rising to fever pitch. People are really staring now, someone is fetching a policeman, and I don't know what to do. I run off across the concourse, and find Adam by the chocolate machine.

We try our best not to watch from about fifty feet away as my mum hits my dad with her bag – hard, in the side of the face, like she means it. He's shouting and swearing as he receives the blow, trying to grab her hair and pulling her, then pushing her away violently.

'You leave me with *nothing!* You fuck off and leave,

and now you want to take the kids, and you leave me with *nothing!*'

There's a fist fight. I can hear it, even though Adam tries to turn my back to it and lead me away. We end up at the top of the stairs leading back down to the Underground.

'Let's go down there,' he says. 'I saw a West Ham poster, by the ticket machines. I really did. Come on!'

But I won't move.

Everybody stares at Adam and me, cowering by the machines, and at the two adults screaming at each other, ten yards away. And I mean *screaming*. My mother's all: '…fuck you and fuck her, and fuck everything! I might as well kill myself, I've got NOTHING! You've left me with nothing, do you understand? FUCKING NOTHING! Do you want me to stick my head in the gas oven? WELL, DO YOU?'

Some people shuffle by, others stop. They don't do anything when my mum throws punches at my dad, but when he tries to defend himself they seem to want to react. He's holding up his arms, they're getting caught in her fists as the blows rain down, and it looks as though he's fighting back. He calls her a bitch and at this point one of the ticket collectors tries to step in. My mum turns on him, and tells him to fuck off and mind his own sodding business. The crowd that's gathered takes in an audible, collective breath – I don't know whether it's pity or contempt in their eyes. An older lady with too much make-up on comes up to ask us if we're all right, and Adam says: 'Yeah, we're OK...' but he's so embarrassed that he won't look at the lady, and she has to ask twice. Then she says:

'Do you want me to take you both for a drink or something, while your parents sort out their little difficulty?'

Adam says no, although he's dying to let her take us away – anywhere. I see the lady turn and look back to where the light is, and then she just shakes her head and slowly walks away. Adam says to me: 'I heard Charlie George scored again over at Highbury. I saw it on the back of the paper.'

A policeman brings our parents over to fetch us. We're taken up and out onto the street, and into Bishopsgate police station. I walk in with my head down, staring at the backs of Adam's trainers – I know I'm supposed to feel ashamed of what is happening, and I do. Adam and I want parents who behave like Caractacus Potts and Truly Scrumptious in *Chitty Chitty Bang Bang*, but the way our mum and dad go on at each other, in front of everyone, makes us feel truly worthless. And somehow it's like it's our fault; we get what we deserve. Maybe that's why we have to live out at the fag end of the Liverpool Street line. Perhaps that's why Dad has left us marooned out there, while he enjoys the high life in Hampstead.

Then again, we're not entirely stupid. Intuition tells us

we're being mistreated – we're not supposed to have to hold on to each other on a station platform and watch our parents scrap like dogs. It not only fills us with shame, it frightens us too. Because if Mum and Dad are at war, where does it leave us?

My friend Richard has told me more than once that we'll have to go into care, into a children's home, and I'm starting to believe him. He says we wouldn't get any pocket money, and we wouldn't even be allowed to take our bikes. Plus, there will be blokes smelling of Brut cologne coming to interfere with us in the night. I remember saying to him: 'Well maybe we could live in one of the lorry trailers, in the field in your garden. What do you say?'

'No! My dad'd go nuts if he found you – he's dead particular about his trailers. He pays them girls from Canvey Island ten shillings an hour to come and clean them every Saturday morning. Why would he let a care home boy doss in them? And think about it, where are you gonna piss?' he tells me.

My favourite song of the day is Gilbert O'Sullivan's 'Nothing Rhymed'. I recite the words to Adam while we're waiting in the side room of Bishopsgate police station – I've learned them from his magazine, *Stars On 45*. He looks at me blankly, then says: 'You can borrow my magazines whenever you like, Tom. I don't mind at all and I'll never cause any trouble about it.'

After an hour, a WPC comes in and asks if we'd like a tour of the police station. Looking down at our trainers, we both say no.

'Are you sure? I could take you in the cells and show you the handcuffs we use, and everything.'

Neither of us replies. Eventually she goes away, telling us she's going to get crayons and paper for us to draw on, but she never comes back. We sit there, trying not to want to pee, or fall asleep. The strip lights blink on and off. Footsteps go by in the corridors. Drunks sing, policemen clock in and clock off and swear at each other. The hard clang of cell doors from afar. I take the rolled-up Spurs programme from my pocket and spend five minutes flattening it out. Then, without looking up at my brother, I ask him: 'Do you think Martin Chivers might be an alien, with them ears?'

EXETER & BEYOND, 1980–95

Do you remember me?

In the summer of 1995 I am sitting alone in my house in London. It's a Saturday night, the TV is on. I write a short letter:

'Dear Nic, Do you remember me? I remember you. Call me?'

I haven't seen or heard from her in five years. The last time we met was in 1990, a week before my wedding. I had needed then just to see her, to make absolutely sure there really and truly was no spark, and that I wasn't making the biggest mistake of my life marrying somebody else.

We met for lunch at Cranks in Marshall Street, Soho. She was beautiful, with long dark brown hair, clear sea-green eyes, and a perpetual smile. She told me she was living with her long-term boyfriend from university; she seemed very happy. The rest of the conversation, the rest of that lunchtime, was irrelevant. Although I think I knew, deep down, that I loved her, there was no reason to declare it because she was perfectly secure in her relationship, and I was just a week away from getting married. As beautiful as she was, I had to walk away.

My soon-to-be first wife Susan and I had been seeing each other since we were fifteen. We were as close as brother and sister. There was no way I was going to throw that away for this unreciprocated infatuation with a girl I'd met at university, years before, a girl I hardly knew at all.

I first became aware of Nic in 1980, the year I started my English and French degree at Exeter University. She was a part of a group of friends I knew a little, people I bumped into at the coffee bar, and through the student drama group. I was very keen on acting at that time and found it relatively easy to get good parts in student theatre productions. And from the moment I came into contact with Nic, I knew I was in trouble.

It was the first serious complication of my life. I believe I fell in love with her, without really speaking or getting to know her. Because of the commitment I had made to Susan, I went out of my way to avoid meeting Nic on campus, afraid of the feelings she inspired in me. But I saw her around every corner, at the back of every room. Her presence, the very mention of her name, made me quiver inside with fear and excitement.

We acted in a Greek play together; I was captivated by her performance, but I only watched from the wings and avoided her in rehearsals. We went to the same parties, and I always managed to find someone in another room to talk to. The strategy worked fine. My acting was evidently efficient, and I managed to convince everyone that I was indifferent to Nic. Except myself.

At the end of that lunchtime reunion at Cranks, Nic and I went our separate ways. She went back to pore over books in the Classical Institute, researching ancient Rome, while I returned to my job in a bank, reassured that she had given me no sign of encouragement. I knew now that marrying Susan was the right thing, the only thing to do, so I resolved to bury my feelings and hurtled into marriage to my school sweetheart, settling for everything that was predictable, secure, steady and safe.

It was typical that neither Nic nor I could be open about the situation, nor our feelings for each other. We were both in our mid-twenties. Emotionally speaking, we were barely formed. But from my vantage point now, nearly twenty-five years later, I feel ashamed and angry at my inability to be candid with her at that lunchtime meeting. If only I'd had the courage to come right out with it, to tell her I loved her. All I had to do was to reach out a hand across a restaurant table, look her in the eye, and speak the words my heart had been saying. But I said nothing. I was stoical, cool, very *English* about it. This meeting was the crossroads of my life, and I walked away from it.

Five years later, I found myself alone. I'd been single for three months or more at this point because Susan had left. With no warning, no discussion, she just upped and left. One day I came home from work and she'd gone. I didn't know if there was someone else. As a senior civil servant, she had her own rather intense work life and a number of experienced male colleagues in high-profile roles in Westminster and Whitehall. If she'd turned to one of them for emotional support while I was distracted by difficulties at work and (in truth) by my residual obsession with Nic – it'd hardly be surprising.

I was left alone to consider it all, rattling around in our 1930s semi in Twickenham. It distressed me a great deal to have such a long relationship with Susan terminated so abruptly. Without enthusiasm, I did what I could to try and restore it but to no avail. So I threw myself into work, travelled a little, made efforts to be positive and to cut ties with the past. I tried to get used to being alone.

I drove to and from work at the bank, putting on my suit and tie every day, coming home to clean the house. Everything was ordered, sober and clean – keeping house, shopping for food, working late at the office. I enjoyed my work, meeting bank clients and writing credit applications for million pound loans, but it was hardly fulfilling. Late into the night I would sit and write short stories, songs. I would think to myself, *I've got a lot to give, but no-one to give it to.*

Increasingly, I found myself thinking about Nic. My grandad died that year after a short illness and amongst the debris in the house we used to share with him my sister Nina found The Exeter University List for 1980, which included an old address for Nic's parents, so I found myself sitting in front of the TV, writing that card, putting it in an envelope and sending it out. As it turns out, her parents had moved, but the card was forwarded to them in Devon. They then passed it on to Nic, eventually reaching her at the office of the business she ran in Clarendon Park, Leicester, where she made videos and short films for business and music promos.

Nic rings me and the next day, I'm on the road, driving one hundred miles to meet her, from London to Leicester. It's a Sunday, springtime, moving into early summer. I park right outside Leicester railway station, as Nic suggested on the phone. My car is an 'A' registered Austin Maestro: way too old to be cool, inherited from a deceased uncle of Susan's, complete with thick furry carpets and a brown leather holdall full of useful spares in the back. Not the kind of vehicle likely to impress a girl.

She meets me under a colonnade of stone arches. There's a sense of excitement all about her, as if our meeting is in some way important. She's exactly the same height as me, and as I greet her and we exchange a polite kiss on either cheek, the feeling of her close to me is just right, with no awkwardness, nothing forced, everything calm and natural. For the first time ever in her presence, I am relaxed, carefree and happy. I take her to my car — and she laughs. This is a good sign.

We drive to Warwick. It's a place I know a little, from an acting job a few years back, when I'd been touring. After university, I'd trained at drama school in London, then spent three years as a jobbing actor, and this had included a short stint performing in theatre-in-education in Warwickshire. Anyway, it's less than an hour away in the car and it's a sunny day. In the car we talk about what we're doing in our jobs and about old mutual friends. When we get to Warwick, we walk in the park. We find a place to sit outside and have lunch. I cannot stop talking. There's something incredibly exciting about the look in Nic's eyes, about the light in her smile. She's patient, listens to my chattering nonsense calmly, and humours me.

I drive her back to Leicester, all the way to her flat. It's in the eaves of a beautiful brownstone house and full of quirky colour and simple furniture. There's a sense of self-containment and private quietness. I feel privileged to be there.

After so many years, and with all complications dispensed with, we are finally alone together.

Sunday turns into Monday, but I don't go home.

✴

The first of months of our relationship were a little crazy. Nic was constantly travelling for work, her phone was always ringing, her plans constantly changing. I'd get calls late at night at the house in Twickenham, from far-off places. Then, suddenly, she'd arrive outside, in her red Audi, exhausted from some film shoot or other, hungry for a meal. It was always so exciting to see her, and I found it pretty easy to enter into the swing of this lifestyle. Suddenly my empty house and my dull life were full of love, colour and conversation.

Nic's dad Fred was one of fourteen children who grew up in Peckham, south-east London, and at that time he was seriously ill in hospital with leukaemia. I met him only once as he died within a few weeks of Nic and I seeing each other again. The contrast between the joy of our new relationship and the overwhelming sadness of Nic's Dad dying lent an extraordinary atmosphere to the whole summer. There was a sudden intensity to the support I needed to offer but I was greatly impressed with how Nic coped – it spoke of enormous reserves of inner strength.

As we drove down to see Nic's mum Jean in Devon, I was

introduced to her large extended family and immediately felt part of everything, like I finally belonged.

★

Nic has a powerful dynamic that says yes to everything. Four or five weeks after we'd start seeing each other, I said, 'How about a holiday together?' She said yes and within twenty-four hours we were flying to Africa. I said, 'Maybe we should move in together?' She said, 'Yeah, why not?' – and a few weeks later, I'd quit my job, sold my house in Twickenham, and was climbing the stairs to her flat in the eaves in Leicester.

One Saturday morning, a few weeks later, we got in the car and drove from Leicester out to Oakham, a small English market town with an old-fashioned high street, a level crossing for the railway, a posh private school, and lots of small cafes. Basically, at this point, we were just looking for a nice tea shop and a day out. Nothing more. It takes about forty minutes from Leicester, and it's like escaping into another world. Nic showed me Hambleton, a gorgeous village out on a long peninsula jutting into the middle of the Rutland Water, a large inland lake. We drove for two miles across the flat farmland plain before entering the village with its quaint pub on the left, church on the right, and a small collection of chocolate box, picture book cottages, slumbering in summer silence. Beyond, across from an enormous oak tree, was Post Office Cottage. The building was divided into three houses and in the garden of the middle property stood a 'For Sale' sign.

Nic and I exchanged a look.

In that instant, in that place, there was the sudden realisation that something huge was happening. A sense that Fate was intervening directly in our lives. The wheels turned, the gears clicked, a dream was suddenly born. And we sensed it. There was something extraordinary about this place.

'Let's buy it,' I said.

Nic, of course, said 'Yes!'

Everything worked between us, never a cross word. Our love is like a river: we jump into it, and it carries us away.

GRACE

G race was born on 25 March 1997. She came into the world early on a cold spring morning and I had to drive quickly through the countryside before dawn to be in time to see it all happen. From the moment I saw her, Grace was spellbinding. She was tiny, loud and strong, with an enormous strength of character, all fists and frowns. I hadn't been expecting it. She seemed immediately to be very aware of her surroundings, and of her place in the world.

The fact of there being three of us changed things instantly. Even in the hospital, it was clear that they would no longer be the same. Taking Grace home to Hambleton a day or two later was one of those unique and unforgettable moments. We took to the feeding routine relatively quickly: to the disturbed nights, all the changing of nappies, the disruption.

The cottage felt even more like a home – with the appearance of baby paraphernalia, small toys and storybooks, the atmosphere was softened and sweetened.

There was, however, one cloud on the horizon. I began work at a corporate banking office in Leicester when I moved up to live with Nic and just before Grace was born, I had been promoted to Administration Manager. It was beyond the limits of my ability and I was struggling. Despite putting in twelve- and thirteen-hour days, the results were just not coming. As small mistakes accumulated, so too did the pressure. It became overwhelming.

Nic, meanwhile, was already starting to do small bits of work again, writing script copy as a freelancer, and the demands for her skills just kept on coming. She hardly had a month to draw breath after giving birth to Grace, then the next job request rolled in. Time and again she was having to turn down requests for her to travel to direct conference events and videos despite the fact that, as a freelancer, she could sometimes earn double in a fortnight what I would take home at the end of a gruelling month. We obviously needed one of us at home to look after Grace. I was definitely suffering from the daily humiliating routine at the bank while Nic was itching to get back to work. The answer seemed obvious.

'You could quit tomorrow,' she said. 'Leave the bank behind. I can cover everything, we can do it together.'

'What should I do about the job?' I asked Grace, who was staring wide-eyed at ospreys skimming the lake at the bottom of Hambleton Hill. At this point she was barely six months old. We were on one of our afternoon strolls, she propped up in her pram, cosseted in a soft wool blanket, wearing a knitted hat. I remember her stretching, arching her back and yawning with her fists reaching upward, as if there was something to grab in the sky.

'OK then,' I said. 'Thanks. Yes. I'll do that.'

✦

I found myself in a whole new life. Grace took me to new places, to church halls in Oakham itself, and in the smaller villages of Langham and Somerby. There were parent and toddler coffee mornings, and I was generally the only dad. The vicar knew everybody, and, against all expectations, quickly became my friend, chatting away nineteen to the dozen, while in the corner of the room Grace crawled headlong into seven kinds of mischief. I soon learned to relax.

During those early weeks when I was left alone as Grace's sole carer, the coffee morning sessions provided all too rare opportunities for me to let go a little. Grace dominated proceedings in a way that takes me aback when I think of it now. Both Nic and I are by nature quite shy; I don't think either of us had been expecting to produce a prima donna. But Grace just lit up every room as soon as she entered it, and still does. She is loud, bold, active and strong. Everyone remarks on it, and I just sit back in wonder. Looking back, with our new, unfamiliar location and those generally amazing, happy circumstances, the overall effect was quite dream-like.

I began to combine looking after Grace with a few work assignments. Sometimes it involved writing scripts for Nic's videos, other times devising and dramatising concepts for corporate presentations at conference events. Additionally, I got the chance to do voice-over work on videos – something I have always wanted to do, given my time at drama school. I got to drive to a recording studio, rehearse a script, record four or five takes in an hour, and then drive away with £250 (still a nice whack even by today's standards!). Sometimes it was Nic directing the voiceover, so the work was even sweeter.

I looked after our finances and was amazed at the way money kept on rolling in. Nic is hard-working, she was in demand, and she just kept on putting in the days, on and on. My experience at the bank stood us in good stead in terms of managing accounts and cash flows, and I could see a really positive future building.

1998 – THE YEAR OF THE WOBBLY CAKE

I say I feel like sleeping, on our big soft bed, up in the roof of the cottage. Nic says *yes*. I say I feel like walking out by the shores of the lake, in the fine rain, she says *yes*. I tell her I have dreams of one day being a writer, and she says *yes*. Do it.

I ask her if she'll marry me…

Like the leaning tower of Pisa, the three tiers of our wedding cake inclined comically to the right. It stood marooned in the middle of the hall where we held the wedding reception. It was the kind of cake you might see in a child's storybook, the whole thing resting on an enormous tiered silver platter.

Nic saw something similar and recognised that, like the last three years of our life together at that point in

1998, it was riotous, magnificent and uncompromising. Her aunt had made it for us. We told her we wanted a wobbly cake – and that's what we got.

There's a photo of the two of us outside the registry office after the ceremony, maybe five minutes after we were married. That word, *married*. It sounded and felt unbelievable – to think that for so many, many years Nic had been so unattainable to me. When I thought back to the numerous dark winter nights a decade before, in Exeter, when I would walk past the terraced student house where she lived, just wondering what she was doing in there, imagining her sitting down to a meal, or getting ready to go out somewhere, the fact that we were there now – eighteen years on – getting married to each other super-charged me with energy.

In the wedding photo, I am smiling and looking down at a thousand bits of confetti. Someone's hand, to the extreme left of the shot, is reaching into a box and extracting the stuff. It falls like snow against the dark black of my sharp suit. I have a purple shirt and a gold tie, and on my left hand I am wearing my wedding ring: gold, with a central black stone. My hand against the black of my suit looks big, powerful and I'm transfixed. To think of that hand, of all the things that it has touched and been capable of, moves me so as I sit here writing this now.

The reception was held at the Victoria Hall in the centre

of Oakham. There were about twenty large tables, some round, others long and thin, each seating about ten guests. The atmosphere was like a big restaurant, with waiters and waitresses coming and going, taking orders and arranging drinks, and I'd made sure there was plenty of my favourite Spanish cava for everyone. My best man, Ian, made a great speech and I managed to gabble a few words. It was so relaxed and full of music. Nic's friend, Brendan, who looks like an ex-Rolling Stone, brought his band, and in the evening they played a full R&B set. Soon, as the summer night started to fall, the tables were cleared and everyone was dancing; there was a can-do, anything-can-happen feel about the evening.

There's a snapshot of Nic, close up to the camera, late on into the night. She's wearing the same white dress, showing off her bare shoulders and a chunky necklace in what looks like transparent glass. The overhead lights are shining off her short, dark brown hair as it curls around her ear. Her eyes are half-closed. She's dancing. Her eyebrows dark, arched, her lips cherry-red. Behind her is our friend Brendan with his dark glasses, grey hair, black jacket on white shirt, Stratocaster in hand, blasting a lyric into the mic. Over Nic's bare shoulder, I can see a pool of warm, yellow light on the underside of the drummer's cymbal.

It was all over far too quickly. The whole day had

brought me closer to my immediate family and I felt sad to be walking out on them – on my brother Adam, for example, who had travelled all the way from Australia to be there. I was so happy he'd made it. Adam was such a great brother to me, so funny, so great to be with. He was a graphic designer and an actor, very talented, very outgoing. It was so fantastic to have him back in the UK, and at our wedding. He really was the life and soul.

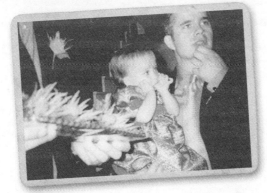

There's also a picture of Grace at our wedding, fifteen months old. She's wearing her special dress, bought for her in London: blue and purple silk. She has shiny blue shoes and white ankle socks. She's clinging to her favourite toy womble, oblivious to the fact that we'd be leaving her to go on honeymoon, the first time we'd ever left her with Nic's mum for so long.

A lot had changed so quickly in our lives. We were aware of that, and intensely grateful. What we didn't know, driving away and out of Oakham on that warm summer's night, was that soon our entire world would implode and all this happiness would be ripped away from us.

HAMBLETON,
9 DECEMBER 1999

Psycho-killer,
qu'est ce-que c'est?

A little over a year later, Nic is eight and a half months pregnant with our second child. The joy of our life together was deepening. I remember her coming in from her last full day at work and finding me in front of the computer where I am typing away furiously, completely immersed in my writing. I don't realise she is there until I feel her arms around me, her lips pressed against my cheek.

'Alright?' Her voice is soft and kind.

'Yeah, I'm fine. How are they going to cope without you?'

'For once that's not my problem,' Nic replies.
It is a typical evening from then on – making Grace a drink, talking about what to make for dinner.

'Do you think these sausages are alright?'

'I shouldn't think so. They've been in the fridge for about a month! How was she?'

'How was who?'

'Your mum.'

Mum wants to know our plans for the Millennium New Year's Eve and if we are up to doing anything, with Nic in her condition.

Grace calls out for us from upstairs and Nic wanders off to see to her so I switch on the grill, grab a fork from the drawer and start to stab at the sausages.

After this, my memories are hazy so Nic has to fill in the gaps:

Hazy? No, I wish they were. The events of this day are indelibly recorded in my consciousness. I do anything to prevaricate: hang out washing, organise clothes pegs elaborately in a bowl. It's the shortest journey from Oakham, where we live now, to Hambleton but it might as well be Outer Mongolia for the amount of resolve it's going to take to go there.

5am, Friday, 9 December, 1999. An ungodly hour but we were supposed to be getting up so that Tom could drive hugely pregnant me to a handover meeting with a client in Stockley Park, just outside London. Today was supposed to be the day I finally shook off my responsibilities for a massive event in Florida, the day when I began my desperately anticipated career break. But that night, as we settled into bed, Tom said he felt slightly iffy.

'Do you think I'll die?' he joked, and I laughed. This is what he always said, whether it was athlete's foot or a hangover.

In the early hours I wake to hear Tom pad down to the bathroom next to the kitchen. We converse at the top of the wide stairs, and speculate on whether the problem is an out-of-date sausage he ate last night for tea. He's obviously going to be in no state to drive. At this stage I'm a tiny bit grateful for not having to go to London after all.

By 7am, Tom has now decamped to the other bedroom, Grace's room. She's already in the bed with me. Tom asks for water and complains that his hands and feet are cold. His only other demand is for sleep, which I leave him to do, as he's obviously had a broken night.

Mid-morning, even water won't stay down so I ring our GP, the father of Grace's best friend Lucy, who prescribes an antiemetic over the phone. I remember picking this up from the pharmacy and giving it to Tom. I also remember closing the curtains — even the feeble winter daylight was too bright for him. All these clues. Yet I was blithe in my ignorance.

At lunchtime I make myself a concoction involving Heinz Tomato Soup and some rice. The baby is due in four weeks. I half-expect Tom to be prowling for a snack but he is still asleep, curled up in the spare bed in Grace's room. It's a big double bed and the sheets are wrapped around him like a cocoon. I force him to talk to me but he seems distant, disconnected. Can he get the covers out of the way for me to take his temperature with the strange plastic forehead strip that we apply to Grace when she's teething and asks for magic jam (Calpol)? Normal: 37.5 degrees. But he complains of a thudding headache so I give him paracetamol.

By 5pm Tom is annoyed with himself for being so pathetic all day. He drags the duvet downstairs and lies on the sofa in front of the TV. I choose this moment to head down to Oakham to see Grace, who has been with my mum all day. I've been feeling guilty about leaving her there. We watch TV for a little, spread-eagled together on Mum's sofa. Grace lies across me, hot and sticky in her pink fleece and purple leggings.

I wish I could freeze time at this point, take the great burden of our lives and shove events back towards a banal outcome.

6.15pm. The wind's picked up as I turn the car towards the peninsula and drive the last two miles towards Post Office Cottage. On the passenger seat next to me is a bottle of orange Lucozade.

Back at the cottage, everything is quiet, the living room humming with Friday early evening kids' TV. I drift in and out of semi consciousness. Somewhere in the fog my hands and feet are out there in some arctic periphery, clumsy and heavy, cold like stone. This is bad, I know that. Seeing a mobile phone behind a photo portrait of Grace, I grab it and try to dial.

Tom's call reaches me just as I'm walking up the garden path. I'm expecting chaos inside, but when I step through the door, there is a silence so profound it's almost physical. The heavy metallic clunk of the latch, my own blood pounding in my ears seems violent by contrast. As I cross the threshold and shove open the living room door, I sense that something has changed in this house.

Stepping inside, clutching the bottle of Lucozade, I realise I am alone with a stranger: a stranger with blue lips, the same indigo as his dressing gown. I try to speak to him, to call Tom from inside his shell. He seems a million miles away. I raise my voice, push him a bit to get a reaction.

I feels like such a supreme effort to gabble out the few following words:

'Head. Cold. Feet. Cold…'

I am writhing in pain.

Nic places her hand on my forehead.

'You don't have a temperature…'

'Cold.'

She looks at my hands. Shivering violently, I manage to say: 'Fingers cold.'

She fetches a duvet and wraps it round me.

I go to the phone balanced on the drawing room cabinet. I ring the doctor's emergency number and they tell me to call an ambulance straight away.

This is a mistake. We've been planning for months how I was to make the trip to hospital. Tom nearly missed Grace coming into the world because he was sent back to Rutland by the midwives. But something's gone all wrong. I wonder how far the ambulance has to come, imagine it ploughing across country from Melton or Leicester. We are in middle of bloody nowhere. This could take a lifetime — literally. It all seems so futile, even as I painstakingly set out our address. Yes, Hambleton, the lost village in the middle of the water. Stay calm. Hysteria rises in my gut, but I have to take control. Like work, everyone wants an answer. Stay calm, stay rational so you can spot the way out.

All I want is to be with him. The time spent on the phone is annoying so I drop the receiver and take the three steps next door. I kneel on the floor in front of the sofa, not easy in my condition, and shake him, talking a stream about Grace and her bright outfit, trying to spike his attention, which is elusive as a fish. I try to make him sing 'Ring a Ring a Roses', which was Grace's favourite, then 'You Are My Sunshine' — which plays on a little mobile hung over her cot. He tries to surface and join in, but the forces holding him under the water are monstrous.

My heart shivers into a thousand shards.

I don't know how long this goes on for, maybe five, ten minutes, then there's a knock on the door: a young duty doctor from the surgery. The night is pitch-black behind her. In her bag are a small canister of oxygen and a mask. She fumbles to get the tube on the canister, it keeps sliding off. For some reason my fingers are steady. To the world, I appear calm.

We get it to work and Tom starts to respond a little. He looks totally absorbed by another world, confused about all the trouble of having to return to this one.

Then begins the first of many thousand medical interrogations that I will undergo on his behalf. This will become a second career for me. How did it begin, how long has it been going on, what are the symptoms? Again I retell the sausage tale, and the vomiting, and the domperidone (the antiemetic that didn't work). Could it be a reaction to the medication, I suggest. Two more strangers, a blonde woman and a man, are suddenly in the room. They fill up the last remaining space. It starts again. What happened, how long? A long form with contact details and phone numbers and next of kin; the first sheet of paper in a file that will, sixteen years and counting, still be open, and will stand (at the last reckoning) about a foot deep.

So begins the transition to another world. I don't

remember much about it, but I do recall that it seemed odd, as I lay on the sofa in the living room, to have strangers coming into the cottage, a doctor examining me, paramedics arriving. Within a few minutes I am being rolled on to a stretcher and an oxygen mask is fitted over my face. There are a lot of people talking, instructions being given. A few hours before, everything had been normal, and I had been sitting on the sofa; now my life is collapsing into chaos and disorder.

They are still swapping diagnoses, even as I am eased out to the ambulance. Whoever *they* are. I am not entirely sure who these people are who have invaded my personal space, put me on the floor, injected me with unknown substances and tied me to a stretcher. There is talk of 'anaphylactic shock' and I just remember feeling grateful this thing now had a name. Surely that meant it could be treated, and beaten back, and the chiselling headache and furnace heat inside my body would abate?

As a kid in Southend, Essex, I was invincible. Indestructible. I used to jump off garages and light fires in hay pushed down my sleeve. I stayed out all night in woods by the asylum, I crawled three miles through the gutter tunnels to Rayleigh and cycled back down the vertical hill on a bike with no brakes. As an older man I endured the pain of my first marriage failing, loneliness, despair.

Nic is with me, holding my hand tight. She has the

kindest, most genuine smile of anyone I have ever known. I am never going to die; I will not give in.

The ambulance reaches the T-junction with the Stamford Road. As we slow down, the driver shouts back, 'Which way? Left or right?' His colleague peers at Tom. 'Right. Peterborough, quicker. Right.' I look at her. She explains we are roughly midway between two hospitals, Peterborough District General and Leicester Royal Infirmary. I know the latter well – I went there when I broke my knee in 1988, and when Grace cut her thumb open on a broken cereal bowl when she was a year old. I remember the ripped red vinyl seats in A&E and the clientele of confused pensioners and smackheads. You have to negotiate half a city's worth of Friday night traffic to get to the centre of Leicester.

'His sats are low 80s,' she tells the driver. Then to me: 'Amount of oxygen in his blood. Not good.' Tom seems to be reviving with all the oxygen he's being given. He tries to pay attention when asked questions and politely submits to requests but his stillness and quietness and distance feel alien. I try to hold his arm, but they insist I am strapped into a seat belt on the other side of the ambulance.

'Don't go away,' he says.

I promise not to.

PETERBOROUGH, 9 DECEMBER 1999

Long dark night of the soul

Peterborough A&E seems like Saigon. The light is dim, orange and flickering; the air is thick with despair and shot through with dread. There are banks of plastic chairs where (even if you're dying) you have to sit and wait to be seen. We get stuck by them for what seems like hours. I'm eventually seen by a triage nurse and sent to wait in a holding bay. It's a Friday night, so Casualty is busy with the usual suspects: maybe a chippie who's sliced through his hand with a Stanley knife, a woman with a weeping black eye, a selection of loud-mouthed drunks reeking of piss. It's just the beginning of another weekend in one of England's remote towns.

I'm lying on a bed on wheels. Eventually, embarrassed about how long it's taking for a doctor to come and see me, a nurse draws the curtains around me. Nic is sitting on an uncomfortable chair by my trolley. I'm very, very drowsy, half in, half out of consciousness, but I know she's there, my last link to the world. I can feel myself slipping away.

A drunk in the next bay lets fly with a volley of abuse that echoes around the vaulted ceiling. Beside me, Nic checks her watch and frowns. She gets to her feet and starts pacing the length of my cubicle.

A little later on, as an uneasy, faltering silence falls on the bay, Nic goes and seeks out Matt, the nurse. He says she shouldn't be wandering about. She's uncharacteristically irritable, and asks him where the doctors are.

The last exchange I remember before losing consciousness is with a Dr Choudray and then Nic. This really ought to have been the last conversation before I passed away.

A thousand times since then I've genuinely reasoned to myself that it would have been kinder to everyone if that had been the case.

In effect, this is what's happening anyway, as the medical staff took so long to work out exactly what was wrong with me, and antibiotic treatment was so grievously delayed. By now I was scarcely able to communicate or make sense of what was happening around me. I do remember Nic stroking my forehead and the look in her eyes alternating between kindness and fear. The love and warmth in them was all that was keeping me from slipping away.

Dr Choudray puts his head through a gap in the green curtains.

'How are you feeling, old chum?'

I manage to utter four words: 'Hands and feet cold…' Combined with all my other symptoms, this should have been enough to indicate septicaemia.

'Yes,' says Dr Choudray. 'Well, I'm wondering if you might be a little diabetic. Is there any history of diabetes in his family, Mrs Ray?'

Nic is getting angry. I can tell because the way she talks to the doctor is terse and that's not like her at all. She is tired and confused and I am apparently dying in front of her, yet the endless procession of medical staff in and out of the bay seems to bring no appreciation of how acute the danger is.

Dr Choudray steps back.

'We'll get a blanket for you and see if we can't do something about your feet…'

He goes out and then we hear him conversing with a drunk who's wandering around the ward, trying to find a corner to piss in. We hear the drunk recounting his story to Dr Choudray: 'The bastard hit me with a fucking bottle – so what do you say to that?'

I feel as if there's an ocean surrounding my bed and I'm about to drift away. I ask Nic to hold me tighter, and to promise not to leave me. The waiting for diagnosis goes on for many more hours. I am cast away, and marooned.

Peterborough District Hospital is a brutalist monolith on the inner ring road. I will come to love and hate this place with violence: its car park barrier; its plasterboard; its vending machines; its smell, a cocktail of bleach, urine, antiseptic and mince. In the triage area Tom's stretcher seems to be forced to the head of a short queue. They take one look at me and find me a seat in the bay alongside him. A trainee male nurse named Matt is very efficient and friendly. The senior house officer (SHO) looks tired and unsure. He starts the questions again. They still seem to be fixed on the idea of an allergic reaction. Tom is given a shot of adrenaline. This raises him temporarily to conversation. His hands and feet are freezing. He pleads with them for a blanket. Every now and then the SHO comes back with another idea. Blood sample, blood sugar – drink this orange juice and we'll test your urine.

Someone mentions sepsis, quizzes Tom briefly about any cuts he may have had recently, then dismisses it.

Matt draws attention to a reddish rash that is flowering on Tom's chest and on his cheeks.

'Does he normally have this?'

'No.'

The whole process takes hours. A doctor from the medical ward comes down. He orders a chest X-ray.

Has Mr Ray had a cough?

'Yes, he's been coughing on and off for the last couple of weeks.'

'Anything else?'

'He went to the dentist this week...'

I can see Tom's ability to withstand this is draining away. The cold is eating him alive.

'Don't let me die.'

'Don't leave me.'

His misery is profound. I can only counter with reassurance: it's all I have. Being constant, a conduit to the surface world that doesn't seem to understand how very, very bad this is.

Around 10 o'clock we are told that a bed has been found in the medical ward. I call my mum on a payphone in the corridor.

'They think it's an allergic reaction. They're keeping him in overnight for observation. Give Grace a kiss from her dad.'

Matt accompanies us the short journey up one storey. As we emerge from the lift, the registrar who saw Tom is going off duty. Matt looks shocked. I am shocked. The doctor shrugs.

'It's alright. Someone else will look after him, they have his notes.'

Perhaps because Matt is a student and not a fully teflon-coated professional, he shows his fear and is open to his instincts. He knows and I know how much this situation is changing for the worse. Again, he mentions the rash, which has now crept up Tom's neck. The registrar shrugs and leaves.

I'm drowsy and I'm drifting...I'm getting ready to go. I hear Nic's soft footsteps when she slides out of the chair and stalks the cubicle again. In my mind's eye, I keep her body close to me and fret every time she approaches the gap in the cubicle curtain in case she disappears into it and leaves me dying alone.

By now I've become 'locked in' and have lost the ability to communicate. At the very edge of the abyss, my mind starts to fog and I cling to my most precious memories, replaying them aggressively in my confused state....

✹

I'm seven years old. I'm standing outside the back door of my house in Eastwood, near Southend. The garden looks untidy: there is broken furniture strewn across the back patio; the fences are made of chicken wire and are beaten down in places. I'm in my school football kit. My ten-year-old brother, Adam, has a cigarette in one hand, and with the other he is bouncing a plastic football off my head. My sister Nina, aged twelve, has just come out of the kitchen on to the patio, dressed for a day trip up to London. She's got a thick purple gabardine coat on that she's borrowed from a friend, she's got her bag with all her patch badges sewn onto it: 'Hey Hey We're The Monkees', a Jimi Hendrix face, a Rolling Stones lips and tongue.

I don't know why Nina would be going up to town with Dad, and why Adam and I aren't included. All I know is, it's a Saturday morning, and my Dad has suddenly turned up in a flash car outside and he wants to take Nina out clothes shopping. He's come round to the back, down the side path. He hangs around with me and Adam for a few moments, but quickly runs out of things to say, and disappears back to the road to wait in his borrowed vehicle.

Adam looks at me, as Dad is going, as if to ask whether or not we're going to follow. We've never had a car at home, and we'd like to see what it's like inside. But the look my brother gives me says no, it's not worth it, and he's probably right. Going out to the road would be like betraying Mum, and there could well be a fight if she comes out looking for us. So we stay put.

Another day, Dad is taking all three of us kids out this time, and we're at the side door, receiving money for the trip from Mum. We're holding out our hands and she's taking coins out of her purse.

'What do you say?'

The three of us reply in unison:

'Never be an actor, never be a writer, never tell lies to your family.'

Mum hands us each a half-crown and we run for the car.

As we go, she calls out after us:

'Good! Have a great afternoon. Don't give him my love…'

Time fractures and twists in my delirium. A new memory: the three of us in the back of a white Mercedes convertible, roaring along a country road. It's being driven by an attractive blonde woman in her twenties. She's got sunglasses on and is looking round and laughing, my dad sitting next to her. We're squashed together on the back parcel shelf, being blown to bits by the ferocious wind. We don't look happy; we're not safe. There's not a seat belt in sight and the speed is terrifying. Dad is turning round and shouting at us:

'This is fun, eh, kids? *Yeeeehaaah!*'

I have to turn away when I see Dad put his hand across to the blonde woman's leg and slide it up under her short skirt.

★

My mind flips in my drug-induced dream. I'm transported to the middle of an open field with seven enormous stone obelisks in it. Nina and Adam are with me again. We're sitting in fold-out canvas chairs, watching a TV crew set up a shot. My dad, the writer of the show, is giving directions to three child actors. He's cracking jokes with them, ruffling their hair, turning on the charm… They clearly love him. All three are laughing. He suddenly sweeps two of them right off their feet. It's odd to see our dad with his arms around these other children.

A loader marks the scene, calling out:

'*Children of the Stones*, slate 612, take one.'

He claps the board.

The director shouts:

'Action!'

The kids start to pretend they're terrified of the stones. It's mesmerising. But then the blonde from the car is suddenly there again, getting in the way, asking us if we're OK. She stands beside us and says:

'He's great, your dad, isn't he?'

I get a sinking sensation as the void takes me downwards. This is what death is like. It's sudden, like sleep, except this time, as the knives approach my body and as my mind expires, I have the feeling that I will never wake. Or that I might never want to.

MOTHER & SON

Mr Malata, a reconstructive plastic surgeon from Addenbrooke's Hospital in Cambridge, is studying the outcome of his twelve hours of handiwork and considering the results of the latest tests on my blood. Originally his plan was to cut away the dead tissue of my feet and hands, maybe lose just a few toes and fingers. But he was concerned about the necrosis in my hands and feet. He had to revise upwards.

He's looking down at my file, at the doctor's desk, in ITU. It's 11pm; everything's winding down for the night. My mother, Angela, comes in from the hospital café, which has closed except for the machines dispensing coffee-flavoured soup and soup-flavoured coffee, and hovers in the doorway of ITU. She would like to approach Mr Malata to find out more news but like everyone else, she's tired, scared, and doesn't know what to say. So she just comes into the open-plan darkness of ITU at night. She takes a seat by my bedside, slumps there. A folded copy of *The Times* falls from her hand to the floor, then she starts to cry.

We are together again, my mother and I. The situation is unexpected and extreme – and how like me it is, now, to be completely uncommunicative. All those years, she looked after her children in the most difficult circumstances and now it's ended like this. If I could be rational about it, I'd rail against the situation. I'd rise up, go over to her, and wrap her in my arms. Never once in my life did I do that, and now that I'm dying, even in my comatose state I am lying there regretting it. Because it wasn't easy for her to bring us up when my dad left us. She never had any money. Everything was just bad for so very long; she must have felt so utterly lonely – and now *this*.

I remember her own mother, Cicely, who herself was lonely and spent the last thirty years of her life sitting in a tiny kitchen, smoking herself to death. She'd had a difficult relationship with her husband; he went off to fight in World War II and although he came back five years later, love didn't return with him. She had an affair with another man, and though she remained together in the same house with my grandfather, the two of them hardly ever spoke to each other again.

I'm approaching death now, it seems. I've had half my legs cut away, and the bleeps from my heart monitor are sounding fainter, less strident in the night. I long to hold Nic, for it to be 1995 again; I want to be in my old house in Twickenham, with Nic's red Audi pulling up outside, and Nic coming to the door with her bag.

At around three in the morning, Angela is woken by the sound of shuffling nearby. For a moment, she doesn't know where she is, then her eyes flicker across to me in my hospital bed. She tries to turn towards the sound of footsteps from the doorway behind her, but in her heavy winter coat, and with the weight of her handbag strapped around her, she can't manage it.

'No, don't disturb yourself. Please.'
The voice she hears is soft, kind, and level. A tall, thin woman in a long black gown steps into the half-light. She's about fifty years old and has a long, narrow face, shoulder-length blonde hair and piercing blue eyes. Angela sees a heavy silver cross hanging from a chain at the woman's neck.

'Mrs Ray?' She nods. The chaplain stares past her at my body, which is totally still. Then, reaching out to steady herself, gripping the side of a shelf along the wall, she says:

'I was wondering if you would like to come down to the chapel for our service. Our number is small, the form of celebration will be simple, and you would be most welcome.'

Angela looks across the room at her, engaging the woman with her eyes, but doesn't reply. Though immensely relieved that she's no longer alone, she has no idea what to say. The chaplain sits beside her.

'With everything that's going on, you've probably lost track of it, but tonight is Christmas Eve. So I wondered if you would prefer not to spend it alone.'
Angela looks into the woman's kind eyes and says:

'I'm not alone, I'm spending it with my son.'

FREDDY

Nic has a million things to take care of. She's been staying down in Oakham, at her mum's house, but she has to make regular trips up to Hambleton to fetch clothes. Early on a January morning, she pulls up outside the cottage, opens the car door and then comes to a halt: it's very hard for her to go in there. She's ten days off giving birth now, so moving is in itself quite a challenge, but she needs a few things from her wardrobe and has to find her chequebook, so she can go and buy food. But these tasks seem somehow too daunting – to get out of the car, to approach the gate – and she's not sure she has the courage to go on.

Slowly, she makes the journey: through the heavy Arts and Crafts garden gate, along the gravel path, past the magnolia tree that I had planted the week Grace was born. She checks the green post box (the one that I built and drilled into the wall). There are cards there from my mum, plus a load of bills. She takes the enormous brown iron key from her bag and unlocks the front door.

The house is dark and seems smaller, somehow. Instinctively, she looks into the study to her right. She's so used to seeing me there, tapping away at the computer keyboard. But there's no one; no music blaring, no scent of coffee in the air, no blinking cursor on the computer monitor. Just silence.

In the back kitchen the scene is just as she left it all those days before. There are unwritten Christmas cards on the table, mugs of half-drunk tea on the side. There is even washing-up in the sink. The clock on the wall is still ticking, and she can hear in the background that the hot water is on. She feels a wave of nausea and sits at the kitchen table. A friend made this table, and added an iron heart at the centre, with the initials 'T + N'. After a few moments, she goes to the larder, finds a used plastic carrier bag and starts emptying the fridge.

She tries to convince herself that things will get better and that she will not be alone forever. She's searching inside for the strength to carry on, for Grace and for the baby soon to be born. On the mantelpiece she spots a photo: a black and white actor's head shot she took a few weeks earlier, in the gleaming autumn sunshine, outside the church in Hambleton. A declaration that I'm going to throw myself into supporting my family so that she can take some time off to enjoy the arrival of our baby. She screams at my image: 'FUCK YOU!'

The silence comes back like an Arctic slap.

Later in the day, Nic drives the forty miles to Peterborough for yet another sad conversation with one of the ITU doctors. She sits in a plastic bucket seat, uncomfortable, tired and wretched, and asks:

'When will Tom come round?'

'We think it's for the best if we keep your husband sedated for a further period.'

'But the surgery was successful, right?'

'To a point. The procedure went well, but this is very early in a long process…'

Nic starts to get angry inside, and goes quiet. From the look on the doctor's face – from that tight little smile, from the fear at the back of his eyes – she starts to understand the grim reality.

'You're saying he has to have more cut off?'

Another expensive pen is proffered; a Consent to Surgery form turned the right way round for her to sign. Nic feels another storey of her life collapsing.

★

My son Freddie isn't in a hurry to make an appearance, possibly feeling the circumstances for his debut aren't as propitious as they might be. By the time he's ready to arrive – on 17th January 2000 – the surgeons have removed my hands and lower arms to a couple of inches below the elbow, and my feet and legs to a couple of inches below the knee. That's in addition to my nose, my lips, and parts of my ears.

Nic eventually goes into labour a couple of car parks away from where I am being wheeled into surgery for more revisions. At this point, her mum Jean and the midwife are the only people she has to cling to, and all she can think of is getting through the immediate physical task. There is no time to try and rationalize, or to be hysterical.

In the birthing suite, minutes away from delivery, she is asking for news of Grace, and then of her husband, from the operating table.

'What's happening? Is it done?'
The midwife tries to reassure her, and to get her to focus on her contractions. By this time, Nic is straining, grimacing, grunting.

'Nic, it'll be fine. Don't worry about Tom. We can't do anything from here, we just have to take care of you. Just concentrate on the baby.'

Nic's mother, Jean, standing on the other side of the bed, holds Nic's hand and tells her daughter to forget what's happening outside:

'Nic, you just have to think of yourself now. That's all you can do, darling.'

There's a dread inside her that I will depart just as soon as she releases the new life from inside her, like some existential equation being solved. She feels the threat of it like a hammer blow waiting to fall – the final devastating strike in the accumulation of cruelty and suffering.

The midwife calls out:

'Breathe! One, two, three … breathe!'

Nic sucks in the dry, hot air of the delivery room, leans back on her elbows, and breathes out deeply. Then she gives out a sharp cry as the pain of the deepest contraction hits her.

'That's good! Again!'

The midwife reaches to guide the baby's head and ease the tiny body into the world.

A stone's throw away, behind a door marked Major Surgery & Trauma Unit, Mr Malata is hovering over my upper body. I am naked, except for the heavy dressings to my amputated legs. The process of anaesthetisation has been lengthy and complicated; there is plenty of work to do, and Malata is anxious to get on. Without looking up, he asks a nurse:

'And how is Mrs Ray?'

'A little boy. Both mother and baby are doing well.'

✱

At the lowest, most vicious point of my suffering, I see my father, the actor, deriding me for trying to hang on to life, for not taking the easy way out and passing away into nothingness. *Will I do that? Will I slip away now from the most beautiful and loving woman in the world? From my lovely two-and-a-half-year-old daughter, and my precious new baby son?* I can't imagine how a person can pick up the pieces and carry on with life, after what has happened to Nic. It's worse than a bereavement. At least with death, after an accumulation of time, there comes closure. Re-organisation. But for Nic, what is left? Chaos. Half a man, physically and psychologically wrecked. The love of her life has been swallowed up in a landslide and replaced by difficulty, awkwardness, by this damaged stranger with complex problems and a panoply of special needs. Add the devastating effect on the household finances, and the arrival of a new baby… it's what anyone would call a crisis.

And yet Nic doesn't regard it like that: she seems to have endless reserves of positivity and devotion. She seems bulletproof.

Those early weeks were a roller-coaster ride in the dark. The initial crisis, then periods of seemingly endless waiting, lulling you into a false sense of security. Then a stomach-churning drop. Pretty soon you harden yourself to good news as much as bad. Daring to hope, yet not allowing yourself the luxury of looking beyond the next two hours, twelve hours, twenty-four hours. Freddy was born on 17 January

2000, nearly two and a half weeks after he was expected. Despite everything, and true to character, he curled up inside and stoically waited until he could be born into a more certain world. He arrived quickly and efficiently, a four-and-a-half-hour sprint. There was no time for drugs. Never has bittersweet had greater meaning. As I clung to the back of the delivery couch the midwife would pop her head round the door with news of Tom on the operating table: 'He's gone in', 'He's in recovery', 'He's back on ITU'. I hadn't realised how much interest there was in our baby. So when at 3.50pm he finally arrived it was just minutes before the news was relayed to a morphine-hazed Tom, a couple of car parks, four flights of stairs, and one long corridor away. But he wasn't able to register the fact of Freddy's existence for another six weeks at least.

RETURNING
January to March 2000

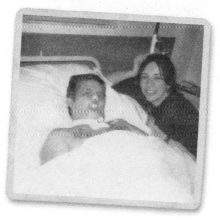

For the best part of three months, I am in a coma.

Nic visits me, and I'm just lying there, to all intents and purposes, dead. I've got tubes sticking out of me. The sound of the machines and of my mechanical breathing are the only things that break the silence. My lower legs and my lower arms are gone. The lower half of my face, from where the bridge of my nose should be, is completely wrapped in bandage. There is no bump where my nose should be – it's flat. It's been cut away. The chin shape is odd too, as if it's missing. There is a slit for my mouth, which has a steel mechanism holding it open so that the remaining muscles don't shrink into a tiny black hole.

Eventually, the light of life and the din of existence return to me.

When I finally come to, when I grip the situation mentally, I find what's left of myself lying in a side room in Peterborough District Hospital's plastic surgery unit.

Over a period of weeks I gradually come to. Slowly, the sedatives are reduced. Fractured daylight pours in from a corner window. Confusion comes in bursts, followed by sudden lapses into deep sleep.

I can't feel my arms and legs, there's something wrong with my face that I can't quite understand, and I don't know who I am. I don't know who anybody is. I do recall that there was a woman who came to sit beside my bed a while ago, and she put the palm of her hand on my shoulder. She had dark hair and the kindest smile. I have the sense that she likes and cares for me.

Occasionally, it occurs to me that I should move, but I'm tethered to the bed by a system of tubes and wires holding me down. There is a fat plastic one, the thickness of a bicycle tyre, inserted into my throat, just below my Adam's apple, and it hurts every time I pull on it. At its other end, the tube is connected into a machine, sitting on a table at my bedside. It takes me a few days to understand that this is how I am breathing.

Throughout the day and all through the night, there is a continuous procession of nurses and doctors in and out of the room. Every hour, one of them creeps in to check my vital signs and fills in a chart at the end of my bed. I can't speak, so I can't ask them what has happened to me, but after a few days my eyes come to rest on a white board screwed to the wall by the doorway, and it's headed up with the name *Tom Ray*, ringing very distant bells in my brain.

It's possible I know him.

The activity during the day is incessant, and at times alarming. There are buzzers and alerts flashing, unfamiliar noises. Strangers appear in front of me or behind my head, where I can't see them. I'm visited by doctors, surgeons, registrars, anaesthetists, prosthetists, physiotherapists, nurses, nutritionists, psychotherapists, wound specialists, phlebotomists, chaplains, all kinds of volunteers, and a lady from Uganda who wants every day to give me tea. Then there is an older woman who looks tired and tragic, who comes to sit seemingly for as long as she is allowed to, by my bedside. I have no idea who she is.

These people talk at me, imparting all kinds of information, but I can scarcely take any of it in. All I can do is wonder why I'm here, what's happened to me, and how I can eventually get up and walk away.

Night is the worst time. Already, I've come to dread it. I hear the tired footsteps of the staff who are leaving and the clanging of doors, then a strange quietness seeps into the corridor outside. Lights flick on automatically, the night sister pops her head round my door just to check I'm still here, still alive, and somewhere the six o'clock news comes on the radio. Traffic sounds in the far distance, and I'm reminded that there are still people commuting in their cars and on buses, and life is carrying on. As the grave silence of the night approaches, I wonder about this *Tom Ray* person; I worry about him. He must have been an extremely dodgy driver to have crashed his car so badly – for there's no doubt in my mind now that his current predicament could only be the result of a motorway smash. He must have done something truly reckless. It concerns me greatly that he might have killed someone else on the road.

When the lights are switched off, at 10pm, I enter a deeper world of terrors. I feel so alone and profoundly confused; I can't move for all the tubes, bandages and wires but I can't call out because I no longer have a voice. It terrifies me that whatever did this damage will return in the night to finish me off.

I cry in the dark, then, and think of the loving eyes of that younger woman who comes to sit with me for hours every day. I can still feel the touch of her hand on my bare shoulder and when she leaves, she kisses my forehead, where the skin is clear and undamaged.

I don't know who she is, but I hope she'll keep coming.

It takes a number of days to work out that I no longer have hands and feet. I'm being drip-fed serious amounts of sedative and other medication. My head is mashed from weeks in a medically induced coma, and the damage done by the infection has certainly affected my brain, as well as destroying my adrenal gland and spleen. The ends of my limbs are heavily bandaged. The very fact that I don't have to get up and pee any more, or excrete, makes me realise that the damage has been so severe, I'm no longer the person I was. It feels like I'm no longer viable.

Somehow I manage to push an alarm button to call the nurse. I want to ask her to tell me what has happened, but I can't produce any words so I just blink at her furiously, which is the signal I've been told to give when I need them to explain things to me. The nurse smiles, straightens my sheets and dims the light again, telling me that I've called her every night for the past ten days, at the same time, to blink her the same question.

'I already told you, Mr Ray. You are in hospital, you've been very ill. Now *do you understand*?'

She leans in close to me and places emphasis on the last three words. I shake my head and fall back on my pillow.

At 3.30am, I wake up screaming. But really, I'm never completely sure what time it is in hospital. On this occasion I know the hour because I see it on the upside down watch when the nurse wraps her arms around me, but often I don't have a clue. There are fixed points in the day, such as mealtimes, but as I don't eat anything, I'm never involved. I hear the trolley being wheeled down the corridor outside, the lady going in and out of the rooms with food and flasks of soup, but my nutrition is delivered through the tube hardwired into my stomach. I don't even get hungry.

Then, there is visiting. The kind lady always comes during the early afternoon. Sometimes, I'm so drugged and woozy with sleep, I don't even notice that she's arrived.

One day she brings a baby.

'Hey…' she says, softly. She has that wide smile again, positively beaming. I try to open my mouth and speak, but nothing comes out – just a sort of croaking, animal sound. Eventually, I manage to gurgle a name, *her* name:

'Nic…'

She nods. I try to make sense of the situation by describing it aloud:

'You are Nic and I am Tom, and I am so sorry I never married you.'

She says: 'You've been ill, Tom. So, so ill.'

'Am I dying?'

'No.' She says no, with a tiny shake of her head, and I see her eyes fill with tears.

'Say hello to your new son, Tom. He's six weeks old. We called him Frederic Benedict – Freddy…'

She leans in closer to my pillow, so Freddy's face is almost touching mine. I hear him gurgle.

'Isn't he great?'

I stare at Freddy, trying to understand. Nic takes him back closer to her, looking down at him, speaking into his eyes:

'Freddy, meet your dad, Tom Ray. The funniest, bravest man in the world. The man who made you and your sister Grace. The man I love.'

She has tears in her eyes, but I know it's OK, because she is still smiling.

It is now many years since the events Tom describes here. But my recollection is as vivid as if it were yesterday. It took weeks and weeks for Tom to surface from sedation. While the process started in a side ward of the ITU Unit in Peterborough and continued after he had been transferred to the Intensive Care Unit at Addenbrooke's in Cambridge, he was actually still coming to in the Plastic Surgery Unit there. Every time he woke up he had erased all previous conversations, which meant day after heartbreaking day having to break the news of the aftermath of the disease. One time, he was convinced he had been in a car crash and apologised for being such a very terrible driver. Then he thought he was still married to his previous partner and apologised to me for not having married me. Finally, he thought he had to get up to drive to London with me, but apologised for not feeling very well.

Each time he would finish with his inevitable question: 'Am I going to die?' At this point no one in the medical profession was about to offer decent odds on his survival. He wasn't supposed to be alive; they had nothing to work on or to compare with. On a daily basis I was reminded that sepsis, MRSA or pneumonia could finish off the job started by the original infection. In the end we gave up asking for prognoses and learned to trust Tom's own resources. As I suspected, these proved more reliable. Every day he survived was another chance to do it all over again.

PART ONE: ADDENBROOKE'S HOSPI-TAL, CAMBRIDGE

February to April 2000

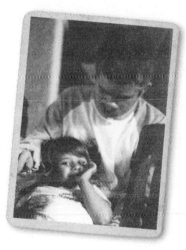

G race is nearly three and I had spent huge amounts of time with her from the day she was born, but now I never see her. My face is so badly disfigured, with the lower half almost completely gone, it's too difficult for her to understand what has happened. She's not old enough to rationalise and she won't come to visit me in hospital. This is a cause of daily grief and awkwardness.

There are days when Nic feels like she hasn't spent enough time with Grace, but also feels the obligation to see me too. So she has to bring her *and* her mother on the eighty-mile round trip to hospital and then spends an hour or two at my bedside, while Jean and Grace go off to pass the time as best they can, in the cafeteria, or outside in the grounds, without either of them ever coming to see me.

For my part, I have no memory at all of Grace, but Nic brings photographs, and tales of the father I have been to her. Soon, I come to realise that this little girl really needs me.

My recollection of our time together doesn't return exactly, but I reconstruct the past, from what Nic tells me. I reinvent it. I beg Nic to bring her, and I think it's then, when she replies, that I really start to take in the full extent of the tragedy we're living through.

'She's too frightened, Tom. She wouldn't want to see you... like this.'

Her point being that I have no face.

Until then, I haven't been able to look at myself in a mirror. I have avoided it, first because it never occurs to me that there is anything wrong, and then because when I ask people to describe what they see, their own faces become screwed up, embarrassed, by what they see when they look at me. My nose has been ripped out from the centre of my face, my lips have been sliced away; the whole lower portion of my chin is gone. Facially, I look like a Hammer Horror monster, and that's not even counting the damage done to my arms and legs: I have none to speak of, now. Just four cut-off stumps, heavily bandaged like an Egyptian mummy.

Occasionally, a new agency nurse appears in my

hospital room, early in the morning, to wash and dress me. They open the curtains, saying something chirpy, turn, and pull back my covers. I try not to look in their eyes, or hear their sharp intake of breath.

There are heartbreaking scenes when Grace is brought to hover outside my doorway, and we just call out to each other. I long to hug her, to hold her to me. Until I can do this, I can't rejoin the world; I can't be whole again, or be the person I am meant to be. For a while, I keep asking Nic when Grace is going to come in – but then I stop. It's not fair of me to insist. Recognising this helps me realise just how bad a state I'm in. I feel like a freak, to be hidden away behind closed doors.

The doctors talk about reconstructive facial surgery, but it all seems very theoretical at this stage, and no one seems sure exactly what can be done, or whether I'm going to survive anyway.

✴

One afternoon in April 2000, Nic is driving down the A1 with both children strapped into car seats, in the back, when Grace suddenly asks:

'Will I see my daddy today?'
Nic draws breath, and turns off the car radio.

'Perhaps,' she answers. 'We'll have to see how he is when we get there. But you're definitely going to see the nannas.'

Grace takes her thumb out of her mouth and comes out with another question: 'Which Nanna?'

'Both of them.'

'What, both nannas together?' Grace is perplexed. It's not often she's seen both her nannas, together, in the same room.

'Yes.' Nic smiles, looking into the rear-view mirror: 'Both of them together. Won't that be fun?'

Nic has to handle the relationship between her mum and mine, as well as all the rest. My mum, Angela, is extremely stressed, tired and emotional. For weeks she's been staying in a hotel in Peterborough, visiting the hospital on a daily basis, fretting, intervening, creating waves. Nic's mum, Jean, has been mostly at home, looking after the children and regularly reminding Nic to take time out to look after herself. For Nic, the competing pressures from both sides are a daily negotiation, and not a pleasant one.

Jean takes Grace shopping in Peterborough and arrives in the hospital with a collection of carrier bags, and tries to keep our little girl occupied in the waiting room of Intensive Care. There would have been a comic, possibly involving Teletubbies, and her own copy of *Ideal Home* magazine. She looks smart, as if she's on a day out, and she smiles broadly when Nic parks Freddy's pram next to her.

'Give me five minutes with Tom first? I need to see if

he's ready, before we all go in mob-handed.'

Jean agrees and reaches into the pram extracting Freddy carefully from his blankets.

'Come on, Grace, you can help me to look after this little tiddler, while your Mum's busy with your dad.'

Freddy starts to cry a little, having been disturbed from his reverie. Meanwhile, Grace is coming close up to Jean, trying to grab some of her attention.

'Nanna?'

'Yes, darling?'

'Will I be able to see Daddy now?'

'Well... soon, I think, darling. Very soon now.'

Angela comes in, looking tired and troubled. She's been to the cafeteria and has brought sandwiches in plastic boxes for everyone, crisps, fizzy drinks, and takeaway tea. It's all a bit awkward since hospital rules say no outside food is allowed inside rooms and there's nowhere to put anything, nothing to lean on.

Grace jumps up at Angela, so excited that she doesn't notice the food.

'I'm going to see my daddy today!'

'I know, dear. And don't you look nice in that dress.' Angela asks Jean where Nic is, and Jean explains that she's gone through to see how I am.

'Well, come on then. Let's go and join them,' Angela says and sets off in the direction of my room, the food swinging in her white carrier bag.

'Actually... Nic said to wait here. She just wants to make sure that Tom's ready for us, y'know.' Jean tries to nod slightly, in Grace's direction, to make a point. But Angela is impatient; she doesn't take the hint.

'Well, I'm sure she would have said by now. Come on, everyone, let's go in.'

But Jean is cautious.

'I just think it might be a better idea if we wait for Nic to tell us if it's alright before we all charge in.'

Angela considers this for a moment, frowning deeply.

'Do you?'

Angela looks down at her shoes and thinks about it. She's worn out. She has hardly anyone to talk to, and the emotional strain has taken its toll. In less than three months she seems to have aged a decade but she's learned to try and avoid arguments, if she can. So she just says:

'Oh, well – if you think so. We'd better wait.'

There's an awkward silence, which Angela eventually breaks by rustling in one of her carrier bags:

'Grace, would you like some sweeties? I don't know what I've got, I just grabbed a selection at the kiosk...'

Grace is quickly up on her feet, but Jean steps forward.

'I'm not sure that's such a good idea, either.'

Angela glares.

Jean smiles and says, 'E-numbers.'

'I beg your pardon?'

'We don't want Gracie bouncing off Tom's walls, do we?'

Angela often becomes icily polite when she thinks she's under fire. Her voice is cool and calm as she replies:

'Jean, a few fruit gums are hardly going to turn her into Godzilla.' With that she stretches out her hand towards Grace, but continues to stare defiantly at Jean.

'Come on, Grace. Let's go for a walk, and see what we can see.'

But Jean won't be brushed off so easily.

'Please, Angela – don't spoil her tea.'

Grace looks from Angela to Jean, but she's losing interest in the grown-ups fighting. She looks down the corridor towards my side room and then starts walking towards it. The two adults, preoccupied with their squabble, continue to argue, the sound of their bickering fading into the background as Grace walks towards my room.

'Really, Jean, what *is* the matter with you?'

'All I'm saying is what Nicola said...'

Jean suddenly notices that Grace has gone.

'Gracie!'

But it's too late. Grace has reached the door of my room, pushed it open and slipped inside.

I see her, and she sees me. Our eyes lock. Her mouth drops open.

Nic has been trying to straighten my bedclothes, but she senses something is wrong as my body tenses and I scramble and struggle to sit up. She turns towards the doorway.

Grace looks from me to her mum, then starts to back away. She mouths a question:

'Where's my daddy?'

Nic moves from my bedside through the door, and I hear her say Grace's name. By now, Grace is in a blind panic.

Looking directly through the open doorway towards me, she repeats:

'Where's my daddy?'

There's a reassuring softness in Nic's voice as she says: 'Grace, he's here, in front of you. This is your daddy.'

Grace stares at me for what seems like an eternity, and I can see her mind working hard to process the implications of what she sees. I try to smile, although I can't really do this anymore. The tightness of the amputated lower half of my face is exacerbated into a gormless, monstrous grimace.

For half a minute, the three of us are locked in some kind of standoff, Nic and I waiting for Grace to relax. But instead her face reddens, and she screams at the top of her voice:

'That's not my daddy.'

She turns and runs, her little feet pounding down the corridor. Nic calls after her and runs from my room, dodging between Jean and Angela, disappearing off down the corridor, past alarmed visitors, nurses and doctors.

There's a twisted kind of thoroughfare that Nic has to negotiate, a confusing set of signs indicating the way towards the main exit, and some kind of green line route, taped to the floor. When she comes around the corner, in front of the sliding glass doors to the car park, Nic sees a group of people staring at a hot drinks vending machine. There seems to be something, or someone, trapped in the gap between it and the wall. An elderly woman is looking into the gap and talking to someone who's on the floor. Instinctively, Nic calls out.

'Gracie?'

She hears her daughter's voice coming from behind the machine.

'That's *not* my Daddy, that's a *monster!*'

✶

I am in hospital for eight months, kept alive on a cocktail of drugs: cafolasochime, adrenaline, hydrocortisone, piriton, hydraquart, domperidone, propofol, alfentanil, benzylpenicillin, chlorpheniramine, metronidazole, ceftazidime, cefotaxime, ciprofloxacin, gentamicin, erythromycin, chloramphenicol, ranitidine, epopisstanol, dobutamine, morphine, midazolam, flucloxacillin, mupirocin, vancomycin, co-proxamol.

I am sedated, catheterised, intubated, haemofiltrated. A tracheotomy is performed on my neck, so that I can breathe. That means, they cut a hole the size of an orange into my windpipe, and stick a plastic tube with the same circumference about a foot down into my chest. They have to stretch my mouth artificially, since it has closed up tight after they cut away my lips. A spring-like mechanism made out of tensed wire is inserted between my teeth. It's like a metal trap that keeps my mouth wide open, for as long as I can stand, every day. Skin is scraped from the rest of my body, then re-applied to the space where my lips and chin used to be.

I am fed through a hole in my stomach. I am psychoanalysed, visited by all and sundry at various times of the day and night. I break down regularly and cry, both in company and when I am alone.

Every day I want to die, and every day I want to live; then I want to die all over again. It's exhausting – for me, and for everybody else.

A lot of people come to see me, lying in that side room hospital bed. There are nurses. Legions of them. Different ones every day, so I can never put a name to the face, or develop any kind of friendship.

'Time for your medication, Mr Ray!'
They come in, usually just as I am dropping off to sleep, always with a needle, which they insert into some part of me, for a reason they don't understand.

'I don't know why I have to do this, Mr Ray – I was just told to take a blood sample. Please roll over now, and tell me: where do they generally insert the sharp end?'

They come with endless amounts of pills, dispensed from a huge trolley. While I sit subjecting myself meekly to whatever is required, I try to think of something nice. I think about Grace and Freddy, and what they will be doing just at that moment, a hundred miles away in Rutland. I think about my lovely country cottage in Hambleton. I think about the pub over the road, The Finches, its cosy back bar, and the garden with its benches looking down towards Rutland Water. In the dead of the night, when I'm alone and everything is quiet, I think about some of the friends and family who have visited me. I have visions of them, and imaginary conversations, running through all the little things I forget to say. These are so real, it's as if they're really there, and I swear sometimes I actually open my mouth and speak to them.

I don't know if it's because I'm crazy, lonely, or delirious from all the drugs, but I find myself clinging to the images of these people, inviting them into the broken landscape of my deranged mind.

My brother Adam often puts in an appearance, suddenly popping up in the chair beside my bed. Although he's a Londoner, he has lived in Sydney for the last ten years. He's always had to fend for himself, and after a difficult start he's done very well, using a talent for art and design to work his way into a partnership at one of Sydney's premiere creative design agencies. He has a lovely old house in Bronte, one of the most charming beach suburbs in New South Wales, two great kids and a beautiful, funny wife. I remember how eager he was, from his teens, to get out and get earning. He worked in a greengrocer's, then in a Kentucky Fried Chicken shop, as a *plongeur* in a French restaurant, then somehow found a way to put himself through art college.

There was a year way back in 1985 when we both jacked in the day jobs and enrolled at drama school. We were interested in becoming actors and by chance or by fate, we ended up in the same college, at Webber Douglas Academy of Dramatic Art, in London. Adam had a spare room in his old council flat in Wapping, so I moved in, and we spent a year travelling east and west on the District line, learning our lines and appearing in show after show after show.

Now here he is, in my imagination, all the way from Australia, sitting beside my hospital bed. Naturally, he's brought a load of football magazines, and he's holding them up for me to see.

'G'day, bro. How are you doing? Stupid question. Anyway, I brought you some mags.'

I turn over in bed to look up, and Adam's gone. Instead, sitting there before me is Sarah, Nic's former PA. Sarah is from Blackpool and is full of smiles, opinions and energy. She has mischievous eyes and a penchant for quirky chocolate. She says: 'Here, I've brought you some nutrition,' and she's holding out a box of chocolate orange Matchmakers. 'I talked to Nic and we decided that as they'd made such a mess of your mouth here, these would be a perfect shape. Go on, lad – get this down you…'

And with that, she drops a chocolate sugar stick down into the tube that goes into my mouth. She seems pleased with the result.

'It's like this tube were made for 'em. Makes a change from all that hideous liver and sprout puree they've been feeding you, eh?'

Her phone starts to ring, and as she extracts it from her trouser pocket and flips it open, she turns away, and just as quickly as she materialised, she disappears into the shadows behind her.

This night is a haunted one. It's busy. The next vision is of a nurse, the dour one who pushes the big wheeled trolley holding a million tablets. She's austere and vicious in her uniform, with too much make-up, and too many rubber bands holding back her hair. Tendering a paper cup, full of what look like horse pills, she says:

'Here you are, Mr Ray. Food for the terminally afflicted.'

Then she up-ends the cup so that the tablets fall and scatter on to the plastic laminated surface of my side table. I have no hands to reach them; I just watch her walk away. Over her shoulder I hear her mouth a single word:

'Cripple.'

Next, it's Nic's voice in the night, mouthing assurances into my ear:

'...and I've been on to the building society. They're going to look into the mortgage protection insurance policy that we took out. There's a chance it might cover all of our outstanding repayments. That way, we wouldn't have to sell Hambleton.'

She disappears in a split-second, then it's my mum, who takes a moment to gather her thoughts before saying: 'Has Nic actually been in to visit you today?'

Angela disappears between the white coats of a group of doctors discussing my case.

My sister Nina comes in with a box of Quality Street, a great big envelope full of cash from the bank, and the Sunday papers.

'Mum says she's worried about the MRSA bug that's going around – but you're not to worry, it's really not a problem. Every patient in every hospital has it now. It's just like... welcome to the club!'

That nurse again – she's back at the doorway to my room, and this time she's flinging great handfuls of pills in. As she advances towards me she's reaching into a paper bag marked 'Burger King' and scattering them. She sings out gleefully:

'Just the seven hundred tablets for you this morning, Mr Ray!'

Nic is holding out a smoothie for me to drink. She's

brought it all the way from Hambleton in a plastic beaker. I can see it's a vivid kind of colour, which means it's probably a mixture of oranges and bananas, full of goodness and vitamin C. She's still smiling, but she has a faraway look in her eyes. Her phone starts to ring. She reaches into her bag, checks the ID of the caller on the screen, and with the pressure of her forefinger sends it to voicemail. As if we're halfway through a conversation, she says to me:

'So the child psychologist tells me that we need to work on building trust...'

'With whom?'

'With Grace, of course, so we can get her to come in and see you. You were anxious about it, remember – yesterday?'

I nod.

'But apparently, we're not to indulge her. She says, you're still Grace's dad and we need to keep the respect thing going.'

Then Nic has suddenly gone and it's my brother who's there – but this time he's twelve years old. He's wearing a filthy Chelsea shirt, he's got his head down, and he's flicking through the pages of a football programme. On the front it says 'Blue Is The Colour' and there's a picture of Peter Osgood jumping up for a header. I think to myself, *Christ, it must be 1970 again ...*

I say to Adam: 'Is that goalie Gary Sprake? Or is it Banksy? Is he wearing his Captain Findus eyepatch?'

But then just as suddenly as he appeared, Adam's gone.

Tears come to my eyes. I shut them, try to concentrate, to hold on to reality. All these people… I don't know if they're real any more.

When I open my eyes again, my sister Nina's standing in front of my bed with a plastic carrier bag from the hospital shop. She keeps bringing things out and placing them on my bed covers: a Toblerone, a copy of the *Independent*, a Swedish crime novel, more sweets for me to give to the children, a comb, a birthday card, a book of stamps, some crayons and a drawing pad, a big tub of Cadbury's Heroes… She's talking at me, and I've not been listening:

'I wrote to your father… well, I should say, to *our* father…'

'What, our father who art in Suffolk?'

'Some posh village or other, I told him about what had happened to you.'

'Why?'

Nina considers her answer for a long moment, then says:

'I don't know if it'll do any good, but you never know.'

Adam again, all grown up, grey, jet-lagged, and fast asleep in the chair beside my bed. I can see he's got a rolled-up script for *EastEnders* stuffed into the inside pocket of his jacket, and I remember that he's been trying to get a part in that for ages.

Bang, clatter and roll… the drug nurse smashes in

through the door, using the enormous wooden trolley as a kind of battering ram. She cries out:

'Wakey, wakey, Mr Ray, I've come with your breakfast!'

I can't stand much more of this. I turn away, and on the other side of the bed, Nic is sitting with baby Freddy. She has different clothes on, even though it seems to me that I saw her just a few minutes ago. *It must be a different day. Is each of these images, each of these visitations, happening on a different day?* Freddy is grizzling. Nic's holding him over her shoulder, and she's doing a little dance with her feet to try and keep him distracted.

'You see, apparently...' Nic is saying, '...we ticked the wrong box on the mortgage insurance form. We could have opted for cover for permanent disability, but instead we went for unemployment. So the best they can do for us is to grant an interest holiday. I suppose that's something...' Freddy is getting fractious; Nic is having to dance more quickly. She swivels round, looks at me and says:

'But I really must be going.' She glances down at her watch, then when I see her look up again, it's not Nic, it's Sarah who is staring at me, and saying:

'Yes, I've definitely got to go. That motorway won't be getting any emptier.'

Adam again. He stirs in the chair, on the other side of me. He says: 'Oh man, where am I?'

'Addenbrooke's Hospital, Cambridge.'

'What, in Cambridge, *England*? Oh, fuck – then I really am late for work!'

'Yeah, I've really got to go, too.' Nina is, for some reason, starting to climb out of the window. 'I'm all right, really – but I've got to be at work in Kendal, at 6am.' Over her shoulder, she says: 'You will take care, won't you?'

My brother and my sister disappear, leaving only my mum there – and she is frowning at me. She slumps down backwards, into a chair, and in a flat voice, she asks: 'Well, is Nic coming in later?'

'No, she's already been,' I answer, scrambling in my bed to try and prop myself up on my elbow. This is harder than you'd imagine, without hands and feet, and with an assortment of tubes going in and coming out of you. I add: 'At least, I *think* she has. Sometimes I think I'm imagining things.'

'Well, was she here, or wasn't she?'

She's staring straight past me as she asks this. She looks exhausted, as if something has died inside her, too. I look away, following my mum's line of sight, through the blinds on the window. I see the flash of car headlights, and hear the rumbling of black thunder, low and wide.

When I turn and look back, the chair is empty. Another new nurse, whom I don't recognise, is standing beside it, reaching over for the light switch. I hear her say: 'Goodnight, Mister Tom.'

★

The sun goes down over Rutland Water. Fire and light sink into the grey-green of the lake. Nic, Grace and Freddy are settling down for the night in the cottage, and I'm a million miles away, stranded in my side room. The winter night steals up suddenly and spreads out fast. It brings a change in tempo, a gradual diminution of traffic to and fro.

In hospital they try to put you to bed early, so you don't cause trouble for the night staff, who are thin on the ground and can't cope with emergencies. A Polish porter with a limp and a tattoo of a one-eyed dragon on the side of his neck comes round early to give out the evening meal, usually sandwiches: processed chicken between slices of cheap white bread, thrown together in some factory in Hinchingbrooke, Hatfield or Hell. He might also throw you a packet of crisps, a yoghurt dessert in suspiciously plain packaging and a drink of indeterminate flavour. I'm still not able to have any of it. Nic leaves me with my music player turned on, so this all happens to the soundtrack of Burt Bacharach's 'The Look of Love', Tom Waits singing 'Jersey Girl', and weird, alarming excerpts from *The Goon Show*. The voices of Peter Sellers and Harry Secombe inhabit my waking dreams.

Night turns into day again. I realise this because I eventually drop off for half an hour, and wake to find seventeen consultants standing around me. A nurse has pulled back my bedcovers and removed some of the bandages on my legs. One of the doctors puts his hand on my penis, then he turns away from me, and still holding it, he shouts out: 'Someone tell me, did the necrosis destroy the sexual organ, or is this still viable?'

A parade of consultants passes by, examining the vacancy where my nose should be. I notice one of them is talking on the phone. He sounds as if he's trying to transfer money between his savings and his current account. They talk over and around me, but don't address me directly. After an inconclusive and bewildering conversation, they troop out again and, leaving my groin exposed, set off down the corridor.

Later that afternoon, Nic brings Freddy to see me. He's ten weeks old. By now, the nurses have hoisted me out of my bed, and I'm sitting in a day chair. My face is half-covered in bandages, I have that steel spring mechanism in my mouth and a tracheotomy tube punched into my throat. I'm uncomfortable, but I try to sit up.

'Would you like to hold him?'

Nic puts Freddy on my lap, then places her hand firmly behind his back to support him. The throat tube is thick and it's painful when I speak, but I manage to say: 'I hope… he doesn't… decide… I'm a… monster… too.'

'He won't. He doesn't know you any differently. You're just his dad. And Grace will come round soon – you'll see.'

Nic gets up, comes round in front of me and gets right in front of my face. She has that smile again. It's wide, and her eyes are looking deep into mine.

'Tom, listen to me. You're strong enough, I know you are. Together, we can get through this.'

Nic appears not to be fazed by Grace's refusal to come and see me. I suppose, being close to her all day and every day, she's able to see it all in perspective, and is hanging on to some inner instinct that Grace will come round in the end. Thinking about it, she'll have to. Whatever is going on in her pretty three-year-old head, from a practical point of view, what else can she do? The more I think about it, the overall lesson of this experience for each of us is that, at the end of the day, whatever has occurred, you just have to get on with stuff.

Nic sips a mug of tea that one of the nurses has brought her.

'Grace will be absolutely fine in the end. Once we get rid of the trachy tube, and the scarring on your face has died down a bit. You'll be like the Six Million Dollar Man, once they've rebuilt your face.'

'Yeah, well,' I say, 'let's hope it doesn't cost that much.'

She giggles and this sets Freddy off. To see him laughing

lightens our mood but deep down, the truth of it is, we're both uncertain. Mr Malata is suave and cool, but we can tell that even he is not certain how my face can be reconstructed. If it was just a question of an adjustment to the nose or to the chin, some kind of nip or tuck, I don't think it would be a problem. But in my case, the challenges are clearly unique.

Mr Malata has a habit of turning up in my hospital room when I least expect him to. It might be eleven o'clock at night, or seven in the morning; in the middle of a bed-wash or, often, as I'm being fed a meal. This time, it's just as my mother has turned up. He hurries in, shakes hands with Nic and my mum, then comes over to my bedside. He's dressed in an expensive suit and wears a beautiful silk tie and shiny Italian shoes. Nic tells me there's always an exotic aftershave smell filling the air when he visits – but of course, I can't smell that. I have noticed that he has a very formal manner. I've met hundreds of medical staff during my long stay in hospital, but none has ever shown me so much outright respect. Perhaps this is because he, above all, knows exactly what I've been through. When he speaks, he closes his eyes, as if he's considering his words extremely carefully.

'I'm not going to lie to you, Mister Ray. Rebuilding

your face is going to be very, very challenging. And, because it is difficult to intubate you – yes, it will be very painful.'

He emits a short, uncomfortable laugh, almost like an awkward teenager. I look over to Nic. As ever, she is stoic, and willing to believe the best.

'Oh, and Mister Ray, your new nose will not be practical – in the sense that it will not function. I can restore some semblance of the nose, but you will still breathe through your mouth.'

Nic asks him about transplanting tissue to line the nostrils, so that I can really breathe through a nose at some point in the future. Mr Malata nods.

'Yes, that might just at the outside be possible, but it might not. You have to understand that this is not something that has ever been done anywhere in the world. There is a big danger that whatever we use to line your new nose will contract, and that there will never be a patent airway. So I'm afraid, Mister Ray, you'll never be quite the same man you were. Yes? Your daughter will have to become used to that and make the best of it. But hopefully your appearance will be somewhat improved.'

Nic looks at me. I make a decision and nod.

Once again, Nic signs consent forms on a clipboard. I die inside, and she waits patiently.

There can be only one thing worse than the experience I am going through, and that is to watch it from close quarters, knowing you can do little to help. Throughout this time, through every long period of despair, self-loathing and recrimination, Nic waits for me to regain some perspective, enough composure to be able to face the day.

We don't talk about it, really. Not in detail. We don't discuss the specifics of the surgery – we don't know enough about it – and also we're scared to hope for too much. We just sit in silence, aware of the sense of bereavement hanging over us. In general, we try to focus on other things, on the children. Nic is a constant presence, always at my side, distracting me with the business of life whenever I get low. She seems to be waiting for the real me to re-emerge from this catastrophic mudslide.

Sometimes I wonder where my hands and feet are. The front of my face, too. After they were cut and taken away from me, where did they put them? It may sound crazy, but part of me needs to know where they were buried or burned. It's almost as if I need to bless these broken bits of me, and say goodbye.

Nic pulls me out of it. Bit by bit, day by day, she nails down all my fears and nightmares. She talks good sense, isolating every negative comment. She makes me focus on the present instead, and on the future. I try my hardest to be strong, but even though I'm nearly forty, I'm scared witless in the operating theatre. As it transpires, there will be a series of extreme skin grafts to rebuild my mouth and nose. This will involve a fat wad of pale skin from my belly, which will be split like a wedge of pork belly to form lips, and later a ghoulish graft from my shoulder. These operations will take over twelve hours. And later, when the tracheostomy tube has been removed, there will be revisions.

The medical team advise that the best way to proceed is for me to remain conscious throughout the facial surgery. So I'm laid out flat on a surgical bed with about twenty people around me, hovering in the shadows. The main lights have been switched off, but there is a floodlight illuminating my face – a great big bright thing, on a moveable arm, that they are constantly adjusting. The light is so bright that I want to close my eyes, but my anxiety level is such that I keep on opening them again to check the danger. The object of the operation is to take grafts from my shoulders, then to use that skin to create inner linings for my nostrils, so that an airway can be created.

Mr Malata is nervous about the work, I know that: he's been honest with me, and has told me that he's never done anything like this before and he doesn't know if it will work. But he's a technician, and he's willing to try. I imagine him sitting at the desk in his big office, whittling away at a piece of soap, then holding a carved nose shape up to the light. I hear his voice from the shadows. His Zimbabwean accent, unfailingly polite, clear and unequivocal: 'So, Mister Ray, I will be beginning now. We have injected your face with local anaesthetic, but you must understand that this is unconventional and we have no firm parameters about the pain you might feel.'

Lying flat on my back, I nod. This is all I can do.

'So it is completely up to you to raise the alert, if the sensation becomes in any way unbearable.'

I feel the pressure of the blade go into my face, and I try not to think about it.

Instead, I focus on the fact that whatever happens, whatever the surgery achieves, it has got to be better than what I had. I try not to concentrate on the conversation around me, which is constant, technical and lively. Instead, I think about Nic, how much I love the way she is with me, and how lucky I have been even to have had this short relationship with her. If I died now on the operating table, I'd still have been the luckiest man in the world.

The scraping of the knife and the cutting feeling is unnerving, but Mr Malata continues to talk to me, to describe in detail what he is doing.

I think to myself, *I* will *get through this. It* will not *kill me. I am a hard man and* nothing *can kill me.*

✴

The cumulative damage to my nerves and mental state is immense. During 2000 and 2001, I am quite literally turned inside out. At one point, after plastic surgery, my shoulder is grafted to my head. For a fortnight, while the graft takes, my head is bent over as if I am being crushed. I'm told not to move, and I'm warned that if the wound opens the consequences for my life will be catastrophic. Then the graft is cut, looped up to where my nose used to be, and arranged in a flap over a piece of bone transplanted from my hip. An ugly, flat excuse for a nose appears on my face. Later, on two occasions, the surgeon will try and drill nostrils through and into my skull, using cartilage from my ears. Both attempts involve harrowing surgery of a Dickensian nature, incredible trauma and pain. Both attempts fail. My mouth hangs open permanently. There's a permanent dribble of saliva, from one gaping side.

I'm back in the room with Nic and Freddy. The truth is, we're a bit in awe of Mr Malata and we're still talking about him. She's joking now, trying to make me laugh.

'He told me all the styles and models of face he can do. I'm not sure which one he said he was going for, in the end. I asked for a Johnny Depp, but he said most women want a Clooney, which is a bit more challenging. Interestingly, he said the cheapest option was a Tony Blair.'

I cackle. An ugly sound comes out of my throat, from around my breathing tube.

'Yeah,' Nic continues, at the same time trying to grapple with Freddy, and to put him up over her shoulder, 'apparently everybody used to want a Blair, but now it's so unpopular, it's on sale.'

My laughing starts Freddy off. He is giggle-gurgling.

'What I told Mr Malata was, as long as I've still got your smiley eyes, then I'll be happy.'

Angela walks in. She's her usual bustling self, dressed in her buttoned-up navy blue overcoat, her creased Laura Ashley blouse, and her laddered blue tights. As usual, she's pulling her suitcase trolley behind her, looking as if she hasn't slept for a month. She is clearly irritated.

'You shouldn't be dangling Freddy like that. What if he falls? This floor's a killer. I don't suppose it's been cleaned in a month. Look at it.'

Nic's attitude changes in Angela's presence. She tries to maintain her serenity, but I can see her shrink a little. When she greets my mum, her voice is flat, a bit sad, and a lot of the life goes out of her.

'Here,' Angela says, reaching out for Freddy: 'Give him to me. I'll take him and walk him round. Let him use up some of his excess energy.'

I try to intervene and to get Mum to leave Freddy with Nic, but she's adamant. I even ask her to put Freddy down on the bed, with me, but she flinches when I say this, and tells me I'm not strong enough. She starts to pack Freddy back into the pram, then for some reason decides to remove the cover for his legs, pulling it away roughly from its plastic fastening poppers. Nic is edgy.

She says: 'Actually, I'll have to go soon, anyway.'

'All that traffic on the A1?'

'Yeah.'

There is an extended silence between us. I wonder, as I look across to Nic, if I will ever get home.

Angela is still fussing over Freddy's pram, trying to adjust the angle of it so he'll lie flatter. But Freddy doesn't like not being able to see straight ahead and he's starting to grizzle, already. Bent over, and fiddling with the catch, she asks:

'Have they talked about your new prosthetic limbs yet?'

I tell her no. She says she'll chase up Mr Malata – she puts in regular calls to his secretary.

'It's not really his responsibility...' Nic is trying to be factual, but Angela snaps back at her.

'But he's Tom's plastic surgeon.'

'Exactly. He does the facial surgery, the amputations. It's not up to him to sort out the prosthetic limbs.'

'But he has to refer Tom's case. That's the point I'm making, and until he does, nothing will be organised. Leave it to me, I'll ring him when I get home.'

Nic is looking at me when she replies.

'Well, I'm sure he hasn't forgotten Tom. In fact, I think he'll probably never forget him, for the rest of his working life.'

'You don't get anything if you stay silent, Nic.'

Nic looks at me. We get so little time together, and neither of us wants to spend it with tension in the air.

She says quietly, 'I just don't see how I'll get anywhere by upsetting anybody.'

'You can forget that, right now. That kind of attitude just won't cut it. Life's a war, Nic, and the best way to win it is by going on the offensive. We both want what's best for Tom, don't we?'

'Of course, but...'

Angela tightens her grip on the strap of her handbag. Most of her adult life, she's had this sense of being wronged, left on the sidelines; the feeling that she has to battle for justice.

'Right...' she says, her mouth set, grinding her teeth together. She grabs her suitcase trolley and moves resolutely towards the door. 'I'll go and find somebody, and let you say your goodbyes.'

The last few minutes of these hospital visits never get any easier. We used to do a lot of hand-holding, in the earlier days, but now, with me propped up in my hospital bed and Nic leaning forward in her chair, we just look at each other. So much has happened in the five short years since we've been together: two children, and then all this – we've been stunned into silence. Four months or more since my sudden illness and amputations, we still haven't even begun to come to terms with what it all means for our future. If there *is* a future...

PART ONE: ADDENBROOKE'S HOSPITAL, CAMBRIDGE

I imagine forward as far as I can, just an hour or two. Nic will push Freddy in his pram back through the miles of Addenbrooke's corridors, out into the car park. As the summer evening gloom descends, she'll extract Freddy's warm little body from the pram, and strap him to his car seat. She'll struggle with the pram, trying to fold it flat, then she'll manhandle it into the boot. The sun will be setting as she drives north up the A1. On either side of her, the flat plains of Cambridgeshire and Lincolnshire will be spread out, vast and uncaring. There'll be some unfathomable conversation on Radio 4, the petrol light will be on (again), and Nic will remember that she hasn't eaten all day. She'll stop off at the Texaco filling station on the A1 just beyond Peterborough, to refuel. This is difficult, because she'll have to take Freddy in with her when she goes to pay, so it means unbuckling him, waking him up, and carrying him across the forecourt. Everything's a hassle now. When she gets back to the car, her phone will be ringing. Looking down at it, she'll see Angela's name on the screen, but she won't answer. She'll just slip her phone into the glove compartment, then she'll turn the ignition on and pull away.

I imagine her back at the cottage, opening the front door, ignoring the phone ringing inside. She'll lay Freddy on his changing mat, remove his clothes deftly, change his nappy, take him upstairs and put him into his pyjamas.

145

Later, her mum will bring Grace up from Oakham, and they'll sit and watch TV. They'll have a pot of tea on the go; there won't be much conversation. Grace will fall asleep on the sofa.

The phone will likely ring again as Nic's head hits her pillow upstairs. She'll know it's my mum and she'll ignore it. Thirty seconds later, she'll be asleep. From my hospital bed in Cambridge, I imagine the sound of the wild, dry summer wind rustling in the branches of the trees outside the cottage. I turn on my pillow and imagine Nic with her eyes closed, just across from me.

I have phantom pains, imagining that Tom is here when he isn't. It has happened occasionally, once at the very beginning. I turn the car around, the first evening I have been home since it all began. I catch a glimpse of the downstairs room we use as a study. The only light in our pitch-black village. I expect to see Tom, head bent over the keyboard, or leaning back in a chair, considering the computer screen. No Tom. I cry huge fat tears, instantly, frightening Gracie, and surprising myself, and my mum, who is in the back seat. Then, the other time, sitting watching TV late at night, I get up to go to bed, truly believing that Tom is up there, already asleep. A jolt, but the thought comforts me. A few days ago Gracie came into the kitchen saying, 'My daddy is down here, he's in the bathroom.' There was such certainty in her voice, and when it turned out the bathroom was empty there was the stoic, 'Oh well, never mind. He's coming soon.'

Phantom pains. According to a documentary on TV tonight these are caused by a brain frustrated that the signals it sends out are not being returned. So it sends even more signals, even more intensely. A couple of weeks ago a research occupational therapist stopped by Tom's hospital room. We were excitedly getting ready for an expedition down to Rehab. She hovered at the doorway. She wanted to know if Tom had experienced any phantom pain (he has – they are giving him a morphine-based drug). Tom has become a case study – the nurse from A&E at Peterborough, an ITU nurse also there, and this woman in Cambridge. They ask very nicely. We always say yes.

PART TWO: ADDEN-BROOKE'S HOSPITAL, CAMBRIDGE

Rehab, May to 8 August 2000

As it turns out the two or three months' predicted hospital stay rolls up to ten. At first Tom takes up residence in the plastic surgery side ward from March through to May. Here, the progress is painfully slow but steady, measured out in the three-hour round trip to Cambridge with Freddy in his baby seat. Sometimes, coming home, we stop to feed in a lay-by, juggernauts rocking the car as he doggedly sucks milk from under my jumper. Another time, the car, borrowed from my ex-business partner when we sold our BMW, actually catches fire in the garage forecourt at Thornhaugh Services on the A1. The fella behind the cash desk allows me to call from his phone behind the counter. Mum drives out into the night to collect us, Grace in the back seat. This, it seems, is just what happens to us these days.

Tiny steps forward are greeted as if we've just won a Cup Final and a Nobel Prize on the same day: the closing of the tracheotomy tube, so Tom is able to whisper rather than point at a letter board; removal of the feeding tube, so he can suck food up a straw. (Not such a great moment, as the hospital kitchen provides a less than tempting squirt of purées: lurid green Brussels sprout and sludge-grey liver.)

After weeks of pleading and bargaining, he's moved across to the hospital's Rehab Unit. This is a red letter day and signifies a sea change. Tom's viability outside hospital is the primary consideration. He stops being a patient and becomes a client. Notwithstanding a massive hour-long operation to reconstruct the lower part of his face using a strip of flesh from his abdomen, the plodding march of his progress carries on.

By the time Tom leaves hospital, Freddy is drinking from a 'sippy' cup and getting ready to walk. So is Tom.

Sunday, 6pm, June 2000

It's difficult to think rationally about the future, from my hospital bed in Cambridge. I've been pumped so full of drugs, my mind is damaged, and I suffer violent mood swings.

You'd think it might be natural, in my condition, not to want to carry on. To contemplate *not* trying to get better, and *not* rejoining my family. After all, what use can I be to them now that I can't walk, or turn a handle, or even brush my own teeth? Won't I be nothing but a burden from now on – someone who'll hold them all back? Maybe I should be considering this, but I don't. You could call it selfish, but I'm still so in love with Nic, and I feel so protective towards my children, that thoughts of suicide don't really occur to me. Quite the contrary. I start to fix on what I have to do to get out of hospital. This will involve a long programme of physiotherapy, two sessions daily, and eventually learning to use prosthetic arms and legs. There is also the prospect of extensive facial surgery, but if that'll get me back to Hambleton, and back to Nic and the children, then that's what has to be done.

I'm still strong enough to cope. It's not easy though, and there are times when I lose my resolve, and my self-control lapses. This often happens when I'm alone, at night, and feel that Nic is far away from me. I have no way to phone her from hospital, so when she's gone I feel very vulnerable. I cry, and I feel the tears running down my face: real, heavy tears. Nothing in my life will ever be the same.

In hospital, they try hard to motivate me, and to make me stronger. I quickly come to dread the early occupational therapy sessions, when I have to practise washing and dressing. At ten past nine in the morning, there's a knock at the door, then the therapist comes in, apologising for being forty minutes late. By this time,

I've been lying awake for an hour or so, getting more wound up by the minute; I've got to have breakfast (a forty-five-minute undertaking) and then travel to the other side of the hospital for physiotherapy at ten. Having slid from the bed into my wheelchair, I scoot over to the washbasin. The therapist fills it, then gives me a soapy two-foot long piece of material with rings at either end. I'm supposed to insert the ends of my stumps into these, but they're too small, so I can barely get a grip. The strip of material is soaked, so first I try to squeeze it against the edge of the basin, then I have to lift it over my head, quickly, throwing it over, like a skipping rope, then begin the laborious process of washing myself – without really being able to reach around. After fifteen or twenty minutes, the wheelchair is wet underneath me, I'm half-washed, three quarters exhausted, and full of frustration and self-loathing. Next time you wash, try doing it with a mitt in the crook of your elbow and without a mirror (hide from it, like me). Then put your clothes on without using your hands. You'll see what I mean.

Our preoccupations were repetitive and narrow, like our hospital lives....

Tuesday, 9 May 2000

Two sessions of physiotherapy leave me tired by late afternoon. My knees and elbows are bruised from a fall at the weekend, increasing the pain in every exercise.

Nevertheless, 'Helen the physiotherapist is careful and encouraging, and I fight my way through, obediently sitting up, flexing and stretching. I roll forward and backward an inch at a time with an enormous inflated orange ball between my legs, hugging it as if it were the future. Later, Nic brings me a special homemade fruit drink, we sit outside the ward together in the sunshine, making and re-making our plans for the future. I notice how Freddy's eyes brighten whenever Nic looks at him, I see how he laughs and despite everything, I feel blessed.

My mouth is now so sore and swollen, I can hardly close it at all, although I have high hopes of the surgery planned for Thursday, which should create more of a mouth opening. As it is, all I have eaten today is tomato soup, Nic's special fruit drink and melted ice cream − all through a straw, which has to be poked and prodded through what remains of my lips.

Monday, 15 May 2000

The surgery last week came and went like a whirlwind, leaving me lopsided and confused for a few days. However, I can open my mouth a little more, so the rations of packet soup have doubled. Whenever I complain about the execrable food here, they tell me that sufficient nutrition leaks into me overnight from the bag above my bed, so I'm not to worry, with a wink and a nod that says, 'Come on, you'll be eating Mars bars and drinking beer before you know it!' Meanwhile, meals are sickening, flavourless and sucked from a plastic cup through a straw. At any rate, now at least I can open my mouth to breathe.

I'm to move tomorrow to the Rehab ward, so I will be one step closer to home. While we were visiting there today I was pushed in to see Dr Kircher and he told me all was going well. He has a weasel-like way of asking questions that sneak round the edge of things, so that all my answers are predictable, bland and tending to no action. One of the other doctors came in today with a new splint for my mouth, a folded-over pin device. It's about as comfortable as a chair pushed legs first into my face, but as it is to widen my mouth, I half-grin and half-bear it.

Nic brings Jean to visit, along with Freddy; for a brief while the sunshine falls into my life again and momentarily everything is right. I mean, breaking the intravenous needle in your groin and waking up with blood running down your inside leg – as I did on Saturday night – is no fun, but sometimes when Freddy laughs all the arms and legs in the world couldn't make me happier.

My diet today – two cups of soup, a yoghurt and two Fortisip protein juice drinks. Orange juice, to cool my throat. An electric fan, to blow away the heat from my body, and thoughts of the future to shore up my soul.

Monday, 15 May. I have just mislaid the keys again. I've always been scatty with such stuff, to the complete distraction of those who live and work with me. Yesterday I put them in the bucket seat of a supermarket trolley. Mum and the kids had to wait in a sweltering car while I accosted alarmed strangers in the fruit and veg section of Morrisons in Stamford. Practically every other day I find the car has been left unlocked overnight. If I'm doing OK on the surface then this must be the manifestation of inner turmoil. As long as it stays this benign, I'm laughing.

A frustrating visit today. I'd been delayed setting off because the thermos jug exploded in the sink. Tom's juice ended up in a Tupperware sandwich box. After half an hour in Tom's room we were summoned downstairs to Rehab: they wanted him to see his new room. We ended up having to see Mr Jenkins, the rehab consultant. A kind man with a twinkly grin, but a terribly staccato manner. He and Tom fired silences at each other for twenty minutes and the Sister suggested I should bring in an electric toothbrush. Mum bought me one for Christmas. Spooky, as I had never expressed a desire for one. Did she have an inkling it would be needed? Today in the car Mum told me she had a strange waking dream in which she woke up to find a slim figure standing by the bed saying, 'Wake up, Jean.' She thought it was me.

Tuesday, 16 May 2000

Two friends visit (Sarah and Dave), bringing more gifts and more laughter. With Nic and Freddy, we sit out in the hot sun, catching up on the last few weeks. They are happy and relaxed, seemingly undisturbed by my disfiguration and for the first time in a long while I feel at ease in company. At ease with the red scars on my legs, although my mouth and lips are still sore, so heaven knows what it looks like when I laugh. Sarah's smile is open and understanding, Dave's is furtive and comedic, and for a while I can forget.

Two sessions in the gym leave me worn out and sleepy by early evening. My diet, as usual, is soup to burn my mouth with and other foodstuffs to variously spill and dribble. A really hot day, so it's no wonder I am tired.

Thursday, 18 May 2000

Nic comes in early today to provide moral support at the limb-fitting clinic. After taking plaster casts of my arms a few days ago, they've made me some tough plastic arms. I have the choice between the vicious split-hook device which operates via a wire sling system, or immovable bolt-on sculptured hands. In fact, I'm to have both. The hooks are terrifying, but stone-age functional, and within minutes I am competently picking up and placing small objects. The arms are, however, far too long, extending my elbows outwards unrealistically, and they're heavy, making me feel like a sad old jackdaw, all out of puff. They go back to the drawing board for shortening.

The surgeon, Mr Kircher, drops by to inspect his handiwork. He seems pleased with the area around my mouth and is keen to remove stitches although from the glimpses I've had – DON'T LOOK – my face still looks like a train crash.

Looking at my appointment card for today, it seems that I've also had two sessions of physiotherapy – stretch and exercise – but by the time I'm ready for bed at 10pm, I can hardly remember.

Juices, chips, scrambled egg and butter... All these people and their kindnesses. Me, caught up in the spokes of their wheels, turning faster and faster.

Thursday, 18 May 2000. An early start to get to Cambridge in time for the limb fitting. Two split hooks, with interchangeable cosmetic hands. The hands look lifeless as a waxwork. The hooks have a piratical charm. At first they are ridiculously overlong. Way out of proportion for Tom's erstwhile 5ft 7in, like some alien form.

Friday, 19 May 2000

I sleep late so I have to be bundled up quickly for physiotherapy at 10am. My stamina is slowly improving; I feel increasingly more tired after these sessions, which I think is a good sign. In between exercises, I watch the trees outside the window. They are thin and tall, covered with a million jade green leaves which jump and dance and tumble in the wind, full of life. The sight of them makes me joyous inside, and reminds me of Nic. Her beautiful smiling eyes. I wrote this letter to Grace today:

Dear Grace,
Thank you for the drawings of us all and of the pirates at the beach. You are very good at drawing and I especially like the ones of Mummy and Freddy, and 'Gracie with long legs'. If you have time, please do some more so I can put them on the wall here in my hospital room.

I think you know that I've been very ill and it's changed the way I look. It will be a few more weeks before the doctors and nurses have made me better, then I can come home and be with you again.

Mummy tells me all about what you are doing every day and it certainly sounds like you are very busy – the school in Knossington with Miss Gibson sounds really good and I'm happy you have someone as kind as Suzanne to look after you when Mummy's not there.

Your baby brother Freddy is beautiful, like you, and I hope you will help to look after him. Remember to look after Mummy too while I am

here in hospital, as she has lots to do and needs all
the love you can give her.

I miss you very much, Grace, but I will get
better and come home as soon as I can. Between
now and then, be as good as you can and remember
that I love you very, very much.

Daddy

Saturday, 20 May 2000

Helen Smith hits the headlines again – QUADRUPLE
AMPUTEE MAKES CATWALK DEBUT – and I
demolish a plateful of macaroni cheese. Two great
achievements. Nic, Freddy and my sister Nina visit,
bringing more sunshine and a helium-filled dinosaur with
a hanging star. Nic pins up a new photo of Grace at her
playschool; she has thick, golden hair, and her mother's
smile.

Monday, 22 May 2000

Yesterday the Head of Rehab took me out for a drive
around Cambridge. There it all was suddenly, the outside
world, wheeling around me, stopping and starting, King's
College rearing up across the green like a lion, Parker's
Piece in the sunshine, a thousand people milling around.

Wednesday, 24 May 2000

A day of a hundred faces and a singular feeling inside. I

seem to be getting stronger and sadder by the day; two sessions of physio interspersed with thoughts of home and life as it was before. As the mist in my mind clears, somehow the reality becomes even harder to bear. I struggle forward in my wheelchair in a vain attempt to put my arms around Nic, only to find that they no longer reach that far. I reach out to touch her and I miss. Only our hearts are inseparable.

She has brought me food so I don't have to eat the muck they serve up here in hospital: thin strips of carrot and cheese, and a sandwich cut into thin strips. In the evening, the nurse jams them into my mouth one by one and despite the awkwardness it feels and tastes like real food. At last!

This is my timetable for the day:

At 9am I am washed in my bed, then sat up squashed into my wheelchair. I sit for half an hour waiting for a porter to push me to the outpatient gym, so that by the time I get there I am forty minutes late for the morning's physiotherapy session. Lunch: minced chicken, totally inedible. At 1.30 the occupational therapist visits, bringing various washing aids for me to try. I'll try anything that offers me independence, although some of the devices are Heath Robinson in the extreme. Nic, Freddy and Jean arrive, then at 3pm I'm off again, for an hour of physio in the Rehab gym. Sit up and sit up and sit up again, stretch forwards and back, forwards and back. An hour alone with Nic before she goes, then a flying visit from Dr Canal by way of a ward round; she describes how they're going to re-fashion my nose using tissue and bone and I try not to listen. Five weeks, she says, until the next operation, while the existing flap of a nose settles and shapes.

In five weeks it will nearly be August, nine months since I came into hospital, leaving Nic alone.

Friday, 19 May 2000. Until a few weeks ago I was superstitious about Fridays. The night Tom went into hospital is framed with the family TV ritual: The Simpsons, *when I was sitting on the couch at Mum's, dozing with Grace on my lap, Freddy kicking lazily on the inside. Tom apparently at home with the effects of a dodgy sausage, but actually turning a stealthy pale purple in the first stages of sepsis.* Ground Force, Friends *and* Frasier *yet to come, a regular end-of-the-week treat like the bottle of wine, and dancing to* Top of the Pops *with Gracie For ages I could not bear to watch these programmes. Now, they have become a link with Tom. I know he is watching them too. We are having a virtual Friday night. These days I have only one talisman left: Tom's wedding ring, worn on a length of surgical tape around my neck. It was given to me like that by a kind ITU nurse. Tom will have it back when he comes home.*

A good relaxed visit today. Cricket on the TV in Tom's

room, and news that he has eaten a huge lunch — normal stuff, fish and carrots. As usual I bring him a drink, and fruit and cheese chopped into sticks. No one fits the Earth Mother / Nurturer role less adequately than me, yet I find my entire day and night devoted to nourishment — Freddy's baby rice, his two-hourly milk, Tom's juices and stuff. I wake at 2am thinking of things that can be oriented through the narrow upward course of his mouth, things that he can chew within the half-inch span of his jaw movement. I enjoy the challenge, and am unreasonably ecstatic that yesterday my hunch that he could eat chips paid off. Tom feels he is starving yet according to the dietician he has gained eighteen pounds since he was last weighed. That puts him just over nine stone (some three stone less than his old 'fighting' weight).

I find I am beginning to get frustrated by the constraints of visiting. I have to be home by 6pm so I can take over from the children's nanny, Suzanne, which means I have to leave the hospital between 4.30pm and 4.45pm. This is getting to be problematic, as the rehab regime has Tom in occupational therapy and physiotherapy sessions for most of the afternoon. Where we used to have endless hours for talking, now I watch him 'pump iron' and pick up unlikely objects. I don't see how we are going to get around all this. If we don't get to talk, we part annoyed and frustrated. The last five minutes before I go can be so emotional.

Monday, 22 May 2000. I arrive to find Tom with an occupational therapist — a wheelchair expert, this time. It seems that we will have to take delivery of an electric wheelchair at home and then transport it to the hospital. Subtext — someone has asked for their chair back. These things tend to weigh about the same as a hippo, and are just about as manoeuvrable. I feel like laughing hysterically at the thought of grappling Grace, Freddy and chair into the car, but manage to arrange my face in a constipated grin instead.

I spend half the afternoon in a disabled loo. It is the only place in the whole hospital with a changing table. Freddy gives up his five-day flirtation with constipation with a torrential outpouring the colour of earthquake mud and piccalilli. As I stand there replenishing nappies one after another, a succession of angry, presumably disabled, people batter on the door. I am stuck, unable to move for fear of splattering the room.

Tuesday, 23rd May 2000. Torrential rain follows a week of suspiciously glorious sun. My kind of weather. Driving down the A1 is more like navigating the Amazon. This stretch of road has become a second home to me. The country bit as far as Stamford, on which I eat my sandwiches and curse the geriatric Rover drivers. They crawl the road along the side of Rutland Water, and stop without warning to admire the view, risking a BMW motorbike or Rutland businessman's Mercedes up the backside.

Thursday, 25 May 2000

Eight o'clock in the evening. I'm watching a blue sky sliding across the window, fading fast, tugging day into night. For once I am feeling full, thanks once again to Nic's homemade food and four hours' uninterrupted conversation. Tales of Grace and her outrageous delight in growing up, of how she roars at Freddy, of how she scribbles on the walls.

The more I think about it, the more I realise that getting out of here is down to me. Surgery aside, my commitment to rehab and occupational therapy will determine how quickly I can go back home. August, September or October, I calculate. But I'm tired, exhausted even, after a day in the wheelchair, being shunted from one gym to another, so I suppose I need to establish more breaks in the day.

The kindness of the nurses continues to take me by surprise. The way they read my mood and anticipate the worst moments verges on the miraculous. They are my allies, never judging, always encouraging.

My legs are sore and red, the skin all puckered and criss-crossed with thick, raised veins. My mouth drips and is full of splint, stretched wide open like a horrified bystander. But my heart is strong, knowing the future will be full of my family and that every moment will be, as the French say, 'extra'.

Wednesday, 24 May 2000. A really annoying visit. Tom's schedule is so busy with occupational therapy, physio, etc. plus a cruelly timed trachy tube change, we barely talk for twenty minutes out of two and a half hours. As a result I had to leave just at the point when we were most ready to talk. The precious last few minutes were taken up with the routine tasks – putting on Tom's arms, switching on the computer so he can use his prosthetic hand to slowly prod the keyboard, reminding him of what food I've brought. It's pathetic. I go away leaving his little sandwich box, today including a gingerbread man nicked from Grace. 'How am I supposed to eat this?' says Tom with a look of amused incredulity, 'sideways?' On the way home I cry out my frustration on the A1 and vow to try and make more sensible visiting arrangements.

Wednesday, 31 May 2000

I'm full, thanks again to Nic, who brought me slices of sandwich, plus chips and a fruit drink. I'm getting stronger by the day, transferring from wheelchair to armchair much more easily and tolerating the false arms for longer periods during the day. Physio is still exhausting, although for some reason I'm finding it hard to sleep, perhaps because some of the painkillers have been withdrawn. I've started some basic life skills classes with the occupational therapist – washing, dressing, going to the toilet, etc. Nothing's easy though, everything takes a considerable physical effort. There's a new student physio who massages my face with baby oil, and there are a thousand cool drinks every day, but nothing stops the pain, or the ridiculous tightness around my mouth. Ask someone to hit you in the face a hundred thousand times with a brick, then you'll know how I feel.

News. They're having another go at my prosthetic arms tomorrow, as these are too long. The night feed has been stopped since I appear to be regaining weight, and yet again I'm to move rooms – this time to Rheumatology, while Rehab is refurbished. Nic tells me that my sister, Nina, is investigating the side effects of Lamisil, an anti-fungal drug which my doctor prescribed for me shortly before I became ill.

Faithless, 'Bring My Family Back', plays over and over on my CD: 'There was a time my walls were decorated, under my roof children were educated, I want my Dad, I want my family back'.

Apart from an ambulance transfer and one quick drive, I haven't actually been outside the hospital for nearly six months. Unsurprising, then, that I feel disconnected from the outside world. So with the kind of meticulous planning normally reserved for visiting royals, Nic and a nurse help me slide into a wheelchair, and into Jean's car.

Watching the vehicles on the road, I wonder where on earth they are all going, where they are all coming from: north, south, east and west; Sunday trips, to the seaside, to the hills. From dawn to dusk, through the twilight, into the darkness and still the headlights travel, still people go on and on and on, making tea, making do, making love. Making it up as they go along. We scurry like ants from our houses to the car, to the station, to the office, only to be crushed and erased by the passage of time. Did we ever take the time to decide where we were going? Or did we just travel, like a paper cup in the gutter? It occurs to me that it's only when you STOP, as I have stopped, that you can watch the traffic of life and see that most of it is just so much shopping. When I'm outside the hospital, I look around at people and see sand slipping from their fingers. I imagine dunes and dunes of the stuff piling up at road junctions, in offices, in queues for the bank.

Tick, tick, tick... *Become the master of time*, I say to myself, *use it, use it, use it. To understand yourself and the people around you. To spring the splint backwards, to stretch out.*

Why do we waste so much time?

✱

In the hospital gym I meet Benjy, a forty-something Cambridgeshire farmer. Like me, he's lost both legs below the knee to sepsis, but now, after three or four years, he's walking and working unaided. Watching him walk and talking to him feels like a privilege. It fills me

169

with hope. Already, and for the first time, I can see myself walking around at home – *really walking*. He says to me:

'Three hundred acres, eighty head of cattle, a wife and four kids I got. No time for feeling bad or thinking on it, I have to just get my legs on and bloody well start grafting.'

Getting up and walking again after your legs have been amputated is a very, very hard thing to do. It's like training for the Olympics; it doesn't happen quickly. The first problem is the question of healing tissue. There is inevitably substantial scarring and dressing to my leg stumps, just below the knee. If you apply too much pressure too early on, the wounds open up and you're back to square one. This is a disaster. If it happens, you're sent out of the gym and back to bed for a month of recuperation. There are also the ravages of MRSA, which can put you back weeks. It smells like damp cannabis, apparently, and turns your flesh to mush, hindering progress just when you think you're getting somewhere.

Notwithstanding all this, I have two sessions of physiotherapy every day and it is absolutely exhausting. The first is with a group of outpatient amputees, all in wheelchairs and excessively jolly as they follow their routines. They are mostly guys in their seventies; they do a lot of huffing and puffing, and two of them keep on popping outside for a smoke. Otherwise, they sit against the wall and call out for tea and biscuits. Once I get over the shock of being in a group of strangers again, it's all a bit of a laugh.

The second daily session is a one-to-one, or, I should say, a one-to-*two*: for some unknown reason the hospital has devoted its two most experienced physios to my recovery programme. I gel with these women immediately. They are both avid Ipswich Town football club fans, and as I'm a dyed-in-the-wool Leicester City supporter, we have quite a lot in common. That is, we all spend far too much time watching useless soccer players.

Anyway, they're determined to get me on my feet, somehow, and they work me very hard. I have to slip out of my wheelchair, down to the wooden gym floor, and there I am encouraged, forced and cajoled to follow the ladies in what I find out later is the actual Ipswich football club pro training routine: twenty sit-ups, followed immediately by twenty torso twists, then the same number of forwards and backwards tilts of my upper body. Then they strap weights to my arm and leg stumps and make me do a series of lifts and stretches. They won't take no for an answer, and it seems failure is not an option. I'm really up against it but it's all for my own good. They sit on my stumps and shout at me, *Rocky*-style, forcing me to sit up, lie down, sit up, lie down... Then they produce a giant inflatable ball, a huge pink thing like something out of *The Prisoner*, and I have to sit on the floor with it between my legs, sprawled right over it, and move forwards, to the left, to the right. As I do this, I can feel the muscles in my torso stretching and contracting, stretching and contracting. Sweat pours off me, running off my forehead, spilling down my back.

There is a *Chariots of Fire* moment when they slip my leg stumps into a pair of prosthetic legs and make me stand up out of my wheelchair in between a set of parallel bars that run the length of the gym. I can't walk forward in them yet, I simply haven't the strength, but I see the point of it immediately. I get the idea: they want me to push myself, to get stronger so that I can walk – *and I will.*

Later, I'll be back in the prosthetics room with my jolly old pirate friend – and this time it's no dream, it's for real. The heavily bearded prosthetist, 'Pugwash', is trying to fit a pair of prosthetic arms on me, complete with hooks. It's actually a complicated arrangement of stump cases with plastic pulleys, and it relies on a deft movement on my part to open and close the hand-hooks. As I push my arm away from me, the hook opens, then when I draw it back to my side, it closes. It's pretty basic, but I can work with it. I'm shown how to grip a plastic biro, but almost immediately I crush it between the iron claws.

Pugwash replaces it with a steel Parker Pen from his top pocket and I have more success with that. We try with a newspaper – picking it up and putting it down – and after a few attempts, I get the hang of it. This is OK, as far as it goes, but I can't use the hooks for anything as sophisticated as feeding myself, or wiping my bottom – at least I don't think I can – so I'm not sure this represents any advance in terms of independence. But it's a starting point, and the next morning, at breakfast in the canteen, I do actually use a teaspoon to feed myself porridge. It takes me an hour to consume the contents of one bowl, but I do it. I thought I wouldn't be able to but the previous night, in bed, I just thought: *What the hell, I'm going to do it.* This is a massive leap forward for me, because ever since I have been able to eat again, I have relied on someone to feed me like a baby. Now, slowly, I am beginning to re-learn the skills of an independent adult. I go back to my room after breakfast, I close the door behind me and I shed warm tears of joy. I'm fighting back; I have won some ground back. Only one small step, but as a man called Neil Armstrong once said...

I am taking giant leaps and I will not be held back.

Tuesday, 6 June 2000. Our friend Sally's birthday. No card. She'll forgive me, but this was always one of the red lines. If World War III breaks out at least make sure you've sent Sal a card. Apparently not. The day is spent in continuous activity. I have become a domestic courier, never putting down where I can't pick up. First, dropping Grace off at Mum's while I head off for a doctor's appointment, then leaving Freddy with Suzanne, stopping only for a short change and feed before heading off for Somerby to meet a friend, Gillian, at the local riding stables. We go back a long way. First, I worked alongside her husband Steve at a local bargain book publishers, where we spent all day eating (and lobbing) Midget Gems, discussing obscure bands and even more obscure American authors.

When a job came up in Gillian's office (Corporate Relations in a large electricity company) my name came up. I was attracted by the thought of a third off a new vacuum cleaner and a chance to work in a smoky press office. Anyway, now Gillian is a freelance sponsorship consultant, with a sideline in building village halls. She also has a horse. I never met anyone who owned an actual horse. So today Gracie, at the ripe old age of three years and two months, had her first riding lesson. I see the slippery slope to the Pony Club before us. Not many people look adorable in a riding hat. Gracie does, like some long-lashed infant Julie Christie in Dr Zhivago.

A couple of hours later I leave Gracie fast asleep in her cot bed at home. The excitement is clearly too much. She hasn't uttered a word throughout the whole experience, just whispered lispy commands to long-suffering Fairy. Must remember to ask whether Fairy is a girl or a boy pony. Don't know why, but I need to know.

Addenbrooke's again, arriving in time to drop Tom's food off at the Rehab kitchen, then to wheel Freddy off through the bowels of the hospital to the outpatients *unit. Here, Tom is having his arms shortened. Dr Kircher arrives, with the head prosthetist. After a bit of prodding and poking they pronounce that Tom is also to be fitted for legs. The moment isn't as breathtaking as I'd fantasised. Still, off we go to the plaster room, along with the student physio, who seems to be giving Tom some real undivided attention. She also has the sexiest voice you've ever heard. Lightning flickers and thunder rumbles. It's quite a jovial atmosphere in the cramped little room. Then before I know it, I'm off again, barely having exchanged half a dozen sentences with Tom. He seems determined and subdued, an odd combination. He's kind of retreated within. I know this mood; it's OK.*

Thursday, 8 June 2000

They've started getting me up at 8.30 to practise washing and dressing skills. A thin strip of towelling with an arm-sized ring at each end, and I'm supposed to push and pull this across my body in an effort to get clean. Then, with my hook arms, flat on my back, I struggle with my shorts. Humiliation this early in the morning seems unnecessarily cruel.

My arms have been shortened and put into a new harness arrangement that I can hardly fathom. From my point of view, it's hardly a step forward since I still can't feed myself, but if they cut them any shorter, they'll fall off: I must try, try and try again.

Mr Fielding, the plastic surgeon, has visited today and removed the tubes that were stuck up my nose. He seemed disappointed with the stiffness of the tissue he's transplanted there, and wants to wait before refashioning it. Whatever, it's blocked with goodness knows what, so once again I have to breathe through my mouth and I dribble constantly.

The child psychologist came today, while Nic was here, so that we could talk about Grace. It's so long since I saw her, but it seems we're right not to coerce her. We're advised to keep up the contact through presents and messages, like before. I'm starting to realise that my fears about losing touch with Grace are in part a reflection of my failed relationship with my own father. Irrational in the extreme, as I am the happiest man alive when I'm surrounded by Nic, Freddy and Grace, but does Grace understand that? I hope she doesn't feel abandoned. At any rate, I need to fix things up between us, so I'll do anything I can over the next few weeks to show her that I still care. I've been pronounced MRSA positive, which everyone tells me is nothing to worry about, but it's a psychological setback nonetheless. Apparently it's a bug you can pick up during long stays in hospital, practically everyone has it, and it's easily treated. Fingers crossed, as it were. I'm trying, I really am. Trying to get back home.

Monday, 12 June 2000. Good grief, I can't believe it's nearly a week since the last entry. So much happens. Last Wednesday night Tom's mum rings from the hospital, 'I've only got one unit on the phone... here's Tom.' A pause. How will he sound? Fabulously like Tom. 'Hello. They say I'm MRSA positive. I don't think it's too serious. Ring Nina, ask her to find out.' Then the phone is dead. I stand in the kitchen reeling. 'Sit down,' says Mum. 'No. I must talk to Nina.' Horrible stories in the papers about hospital superbugs slam into my mind. Damn. I find Nina's number on my mobile. Mum has to talk to her, Freddy is crying, his feed disturbed. Nina promises to ring round, find out what she can.

Half an hour crawls by. The phone rings. Nina, full of reassurance. After a long chat with the nurse on Tom's ward this evening it seems that MRSA is all over the hospital. It means they will have to barrier-nurse him (aprons and gloves) until he's clear. The bug is a danger to young and elderly, and seriously ill patients particularly. Also, it may have an impact on the healing of Tom's niggly knee wounds. But not the apocalyptic scenario that my imagination had created in the hiatus.

In the ensuing days 'normality' settles in again. We have an encouraging session with a child psychologist on Thursday — Marion. She lets us talk for hours about where we are. I hear Tom voice feelings that he's never divulged before. Should I be listening to this? Suddenly I have a chilling glimpse of his night-time terrors. Mine are nothing by comparison.

Strange that weekends have still managed to keep a special identity. Saturday is spent in a duvet of catarrh. I try to get away from Mum's, where we spent the previous night, but apart from a blissful wander round the market, buying a skipload of fruit, I still end up there at 5pm, rolling around on a blanket in the garden with Grace. It's the first hot day of the summer and every dribble of energy has oozed out of me.

Tuesday, 20 June 2000

Our second session with Marion. Gracie strides purposefully into the playroom at the Brooklands Family Consultation Unit and takes possession of the wooden Wendy house. As she fires orders at a trio of stunned-looking very hairy dolls, Marion manages the neat trick of observing and joining in simultaneously. Suddenly I am conscious of just how proud I am of Grace. She can hold her own with complete strangers, charming and entertaining them effortlessly, and, apparently, I hope, unconsciously.

Wednesday, 21 June 2000. I type this entry at 11pm with Freddy sitting on my lap. He sits neatly and quietly and wide-awake. I feel very calm, having resolved not to worry about anything I cannot control. There is great trash on the TV. It's the longest day of the year and I am reminded of how far we have all come since the shortest, darkest day. Nina's husband, Dave, wants me to write my story for Tom's website. So far I have been avoiding this. My memories are quite loosely fastened down, and are normally kept under control by the sheer weight of domestic routine. Perhaps my current state of mind will allow me to do the job.

Saturday, 17 June 2000

Burt Bacharach spinning elegantly, bitterly, through a hot Saturday afternoon: 'That song is sung now, this bell has rung out...' All our lives, all of our twisted turns, deserve their own soft background brass section. *What's new pussycat?* I'm like a shipwrecked man, afloat on a piece of driftwood. Hour after hour goes by, with me hardly moving, my mind rolling over like the drum of a washing machine. Over and over, the same questions – can we live comfortably in our tiny house or should we move? Will my face always feel so twisted? How can I hope to make Nic happy? When will I see Grace again? *Where is the sunshine we once knew...?*

Saturday, 24 June 2000

Incredibly, a week since I last wrote this diary – time is beginning to fly by. As usual, the week's been full of chips and therapy, motorised odysseys in my wheelchair through the hospital, bouncing from A to B and back again at heady speeds, sometimes in excess of 5mph. Careful.

Faithless, spinning around and around on my CD, the beat and the bass filling me, inspiring. Two new things – first, I've got into the habit last thing at night of leaving my wheelchair positioned at the side of my bed, so that I can get up in the mornings and slide backwards into it – one small step for this mankind, one giant leap towards independence. Second, I've been using the proper loos instead of having the 'commodes' wheeled into my room – another important step forward. I still need a little help and supervision on the loo, but I'll be working hard over the next few weeks to eliminate that. Otherwise, from a medical point of view, things are still moving slowly. I'm trying to take as many of the drugs as I can orally, rather than down my peg tube, so that eventually I can dispense with it – probably after the next operation. That should be sometime in the next two or three weeks, then once I'm recovered from that, I can get off Lonely Street and spend weekends at home, which will be like starting a new life.

As ever, Nic is full of patience and love. We share a tough kind of composure that just endures, a protective covering, nature's throw-over; nothing seems to alienate us from each other – nothing. She visits almost every day, bringing food, Freddy and fifteen thousand smiles that reassure and cool me like a breeze. Today she's at home, as our friends are organising themselves into a sponsored bike ride around Rutland Water – once again, for our benefit. Soon we'll have plenty of funds to put towards state-of-the-art limbs, or alterations to the house. As before, I'm astonished at our friends' generosity with their time and money.

Dave, my brother-in-law, comes to visit. He has a refreshing, practical attitude to life and its problems, so conversation is easy and direct, and focused on the way things are, rather than the way they should or could be. We waste an hour trying unsuccessfully to send an email home from the hospital's computer; we talk and talk and talk. Mary, his daughter and my niece, is on a drama tour of Eastern Europe. I'm reminded again how fast time flies – I remember vividly the fuss and joy when she was born, twenty years ago.

The wounds on my knees are healing. Only there is still a deep cut about the size of a penny in the left one, and this is taking time to close over. Otherwise, I'm going from strength to strength: sleeping well, eating well, and trying hard to be positive about overcoming the remaining barriers between hospital and home. One, at least, has been pushed over: I can now call Nic on the mobile phone that Nina gave me. Just to hear her voice, just to say the words, it's as if my soul were travelling home.

Thursday, 29 June 2000. This is getting ridiculous, Thursday already! A few hundred more miles on the clock, more stretching and pinging of the emotional elastic, and a thousand more pieces of food, cut into strips and wedges. Grace is at nursery school, Freddy is bopping around in his bouncy seat, grinning at a hilarious private joke. Suzanne has put one of Grace's tapes on in the kitchen, Old MacDonald. And every ten minutes or so the phone rings — someone wanting to deliver Tom's electric wheelchair, Nina, Angela. I, meantime, have stolen a few illicit daytime moments at the computer. I feel guilty and itchily conscious that I am sitting on some huge bureaucratic time bomb: forms to fill in, details that need confirming, our lives mashed and re-formed into neat DSS-digestible chunks. I also need to find a dentist for the family. Having canned our regular Leicester practice in a bid to find somewhere more sensible, i.e. local, I find that all the Oakham dentists' lists are closed, unless you are privy to some password... either Horse, Neigh, or Barbour, I suspect.

Saturday 1 July 2000

A story I wrote for Grace, prompted by the child psychologist:

Once upon a time there were three little bears — Mummy Bear, Daddy Bear and Little Bear.

In the mornings, Mummy Bear would kiss Little Bear and go off to her cave to do her work.

Then Little Bear and Daddy Bear had time to

play together. Sometimes Daddy Bear would sing songs like 'Insey Winsey Spider' and Little Bear would sing along too. Other times Daddy Bear would take Little Bear off to the woods to play with the other little bears. One of Little Bear's favourite things was when Daddy Bear told her stories.

In the evenings, Mummy Bear would come back from her cave and they'd all have honey tea together.

One day, Daddy and Mummy Bear told Little Bear that she was going to have a new brother or sister. But Little Bear wasn't sure that she liked the idea. Would Mummy and Daddy Bear still love her and look after her in just the same way? Mummy and Daddy Bear told her that of course they would still love her LOTS & LOTS & LOTS forever after Baby Bear arrived. This made Little Bear happy and she sang some more songs with Daddy.

Sometimes Daddy Bear would take Little Bear to play on the toys in the park — Little Bear liked that a lot. For a special treat, Daddy Bear would take Little Bear to Donald's for chips and a chocolate milkshake.

Then one day a sad thing happened: Daddy Bear became poorly and had to go to hospital. Sometimes, Mummy Bear took Little Bear to visit Daddy Bear in hospital. Daddy Bear was very poorly and couldn't play with Little Bear or even talk to her. He missed his Little Bear very much and thought about her all the time. Everyone was very worried because Daddy Bear was so poorly he nearly died.

Often Little Bear stayed at home while Mummy Bear went off to visit Daddy Bear. Luckily, Little Bear had a kind Nanny Bear to look after her and play with her.

The doctors in hospital gave Daddy Bear lots of strong medicine. With the help of the doctors and his medicine, Daddy Bear became stronger and fought the poorliness just like a soldier.

But although Daddy Bear got much better, the doctors could not make him like he was before. Daddy Bear was still Daddy Bear, but the doctors had to take away the poorly bits.

'Which poorly bits?' asked Little Bear.

'Parts of his nose and lips, his hands and his feet – but the doctors will give him new parts,' explained Mummy Bear.

Little Bear asked if the same thing would happen to her or if she could catch it.

'No, of course not. Nobody will catch this poorliness that Daddy had. It's very, very, very rare,' said Mummy Bear. 'Your daddy was just very, very unlucky.'

Little Bear could see that Mummy was upset for a moment and so they both had a little cry.

Then one day Mummy had to go into a different Baby Hospital because Baby Bear was ready to be born. Little Bear was very, very happy to meet her new little baby brother, Baby Bear. And even though Daddy Bear was asleep in a different hospital, he knew that Baby Bear had been born and it was the best happy moment for everyone, for all the family together.

Then, because Baby Bear was so tiny, he couldn't stay at home and play in the woods with the other little bears. Instead, he had to go with Mummy Bear to hospital when she went to visit Daddy Bear. Little Bear usually stayed at home and played with Nanny Bear. She also had fun playing with the other little bears in the woods. Lots of people brought Daddy flowers and chocolates in hospital. Daddy Bear sent one of his flowers home as a gift for his special Little Bear. Another day he sent her some yummy chocolate bunnies. One day, Little Bear drew pictures on bright yellow paper and sent them along to the hospital with Mummy Bear. Daddy Bear was so happy to have Little Bear's pictures that he put them up on the wall of his room in the hospital. Another day, Mummy Bear took a photo of Daddy Bear so that Little Bear could see him and

185

carry him around with her to show her friends.

One day Little Bear thought she'd like to see Daddy Bear. She felt a little bit scared. How could she be sure it was still her own Daddy Bear when his poorly bits had been taken away and he looked so different? Mummy Bear told Little Bear that even if Daddy Bear looked different he was still the same Daddy Bear, with the same smiling eyes and the same cuddly tummy, and that he would soon have replacements for his arms and legs. Mummy said, 'Daddy can still sing you your favourite songs, tell you the same lovely stories, and play with you in the garden.'

Little Bear felt a little happier.

Soon enough it was time for Daddy Bear to come home and just like Mummy Bear had said, Daddy Bear did look different, but really and truly he was still her Daddy Bear. Little Bear could also see that Baby Bear and Mummy Bear were very, very happy to welcome Daddy Bear back home.

Little Bear still took a while getting used to Daddy Bear again. Then they had many happy times together, playing games, eating lovely food and going out on trips.

Sometimes, Daddy Bear would go back into hospital for just a few days, so that the doctors could make his nose and lips look better. Each time

Daddy Bear came home his face looked a little bit different but Little Bear was getting cleverer and cleverer and knew that it was always the same Daddy Bear who loved all the family – Baby Bear, Mummy Bear, Nanny Bear and especially his one and only Little Bear – forever after and after.

July 2000. My daily routine of going to the hospital rehab gym represents the first opportunity of re-establishing a life routine. It is a blessing, just to be expected there, and to have something to work towards.

While sitting on the mat in the gym, I really feel like half a person. Everyone else is at head height, and I am on the floor, unable to get back up to my wheelchair again without assistance. I am back to being a child again. Until the stumps of my legs have taken shape and are fully healed, I cannot be cast for permanent legs. In my case, this problem is exacerbated because I have that open wound on one knee that simply will not heal. Eventually I will get fed up waiting, and simply have it dressed and cleaned every day for the next nine months, while it takes its own sweet time closing.

Balancing in the prosthetic legs is difficult. I spend so much of my time horizontal in bed that any attempt to go upright is like walking on stilts. I feel very precarious as I walk between the bars, with each of the physiotherapists holding on to the stumps of my arms. I take about five steps, then rest, holding on to the bars, then I take five more. Step by step, I go forward.

Then, one morning, I am walking. Up on artificial legs, leaning with my elbows on the parallel bars, doing two full lengths, or about fifty feet. It's painful. The legs feel like lead weights, and I have to concentrate hard to keep straight, but technically, it's actual walking.

For the first time since Sepsis tried to kill me, I am up and walking.

I feel powerful, dangerous, exhausted, determined, all at the same time. I get a nurse to help me ring Nic to tell her. Her voice is colourful and kind and exciting and calm and close and happy; talking to her makes me feel strong.

July 2000

The year moves on. Summer comes. It's been a full seven months since this all started and I'm still in hospital – but now I'm permanently in the Rehabilitation Unit. Every single day without fail, Nic makes the 114-mile round trip to see me. I try to find little ways to improve every day, so I can be released and go back home, but I feel trapped here. Time drags.

Sometimes I close my eyes and conjure up the image of the sun sparkling on Rutland Water. There's one particular bench I used to sit on, with Grace alongside me in her pram. It's still there, down by the Old Hall, a part-medieval building that lies half-sunken in the water, and I often think of it: the afternoon sun, and the cool breeze on the skin of my face, when I *had* a face.

I imagine the scene in our bedroom at Post Office Cottage, Nic is sorting through an artist's box of oil paints and brushes. She bought them months ago, just before I got ill. It's long been her ambition to find some time to start painting again, but she's never quite got round to it. All the brushes still have their plastic sleeves on them, all the fat tubes of oil paint have their lids intact. She suddenly looks up at the full-length mirror in the corner of the bedroom. She sees her own reflection in it and struggles to recognise herself – her skin is pale, her face looks drawn and she has a permanent frown. She wonders whether she'll ever get to use the paint in anger; whether she ought to allow the floodgates to open. But if she did, it might drown her. Better to freeze out any thought of when things will get better, back to normal, whatever that may mean. She crosses the room, lifts the mirror and puts it in the corner cupboard. Then she goes to the smaller mirror, above the little cast-iron fireplace, lifts it off its hook and stashes it away. She wants every mirror out of view and out of use: appearances are no longer important.

Friday, 7 July 2000

Blocks of time seem to fall away suddenly, cliff faces of it, sliding noiselessly into the Addenbrooke's Sea. Another week gone by. I try to keep track of it by way of a weekly timetable pinned up on my wall. It tells me where to go and when the 'Porter Will Collect', as if I were some kind of package to be shunted from one end of the hospital to the other. And unerringly, I follow these Seers of the Way through the gloomy, hot underground tunnels, a pilgrim in my motorised wheelchair. They are Prophets: of football, holidays, pub politics, parking cars, rain and traffic jams; they are the Masters of Time, Organisers of Seconds, Minutes and Hours as they guide me through the day, picking me a path over a Giant's Causeway.

I walked on the moon again today, this time using a rollator frame on tiny wheels, so I could rest my elbows and just inch forward, slowly, slowly. The pressure on the ends of my stumps is still almost unbearable, but if I am ever to get home again, I know I have to bear it. Gritting my teeth and thinking of Nic, Grace and little Freddy. He is the happiest little boy. His open-mouthed smile is like treasure; his eyes are excited, dazzled, and wide with curiosity. I'm so pleased to see him – even though he's only six months old, it's as if he were an ally, and being with him today reminded me (if I need to be reminded) that I am rich, rich, rich. That I need nothing (not even arms and legs) beyond this amazing family of mine, and the time that I am given to love and encourage them.

I feel guilty and sad to be here in hospital for another weekend, because if I pushed for it, I know I could be spending Saturday and Sunday at home. But I'm nervous of seeing Grace, of her reaction to me, disfigured as I am. The next operation is set for 17 July. Then, once I am healed, hopefully my face (my nose) will look half-human, and I can start weekend trips home.

In the meantime, I lie awake at night imagining Nic alone; I regret every minute that passes, every second, every block that drops into the sea. When this is all done and over, I vow to become a Master of Time.

Monday, 10 July 2000. I remember Tom once saying to some friends that he was too happy to write. That was soon after we married. He has been writing on and off for years. Beautifully turned ideas, tumbling, twisting eddies of words to take your breath away, coinciding with periods of strained relationships, loneliness or frustration. I suppose I have at times felt guilty that our domestic contentment stemmed the flow. Now that Tom really does have the emotional conditions that spur him to write my head aches with the ironic permutations. It's been a strange few days. Grace has broken the wall of silence. Yesterday, out of the blue, she declares that she wants to speak to her daddy. Suspicious, I suggest that she talks to him on the phone next time he calls. Then we go off to the pictures in Nottingham with Sarah and Tony.

Sarah was our PA at the production company in Leicester and Tony is her husband. Over time they've become firm family friends. They live in the real world, they are practical people, down to earth, fun to be with. The film is Chicken Run *— highly recommended, even with a wriggling six-month-old baby up your shirt. So at 8.30ish the phone rings. I say, 'That might be Daddy,' expecting Grace to exit the room faster than a dog. Instead she runs for the phone, pulls it off the wall by the cable, and launches into a report of her day. I am beyond understanding. Is Grace any more mysterious than your average three-year-old? Is it the repeated reassurance that Tom can walk, and he has plastic legs? Or did the bear family tale do its job, allowing her to find a place in our story?*

Tomorrow is our wedding anniversary, our second. We are all torn. I take refuge in late night chocolate biscuits, and will wake at 2am with heartburn.

Tuesday, 11 July 2000. Me, Tom, Freddy asleep. Cheeseburger and chips in Burger King. I am in heaven. Happy anniversary!

Wednesday, 12 July 2000. A day 'off' in our benevolent parallel universe. There is a commode in our outhouse — delivered yesterday. Too surreal. I manhandle Grace into the car and whisk her off to Rascals, our local soft play centre, stopping only to pick up Tom's wedding ring from Mum's shower, where I left it this morning. There we bump into some friends from our previous life. They are visibly delighted to see Grace popping up through a bright blue cargo net, and are pretty amazed to see me a couple of dozen feet behind. They are all kind enquiries and concern and for a second time today I am bathed in an unexpected warm glow (the first is when Mum rings up unexpectedly to tell me she loves me!).

It occurs to me that they really don't know how we are getting through all this.

The thing is, no one would choose to live through our experiences, but when it happens you have no choice. The choice we have is in the style we adopt; that is the tough bit.

Gracie is a bit tired and fractious so we move on to Morrisons for lunch and grocery shopping. Morrisons is inextricably linked with our family. Tom and Gracie have been having chip and cake dinners there since she was a tiny tot. True to form, Grace moves straight in on the mechanical Postman Pat ride in the foyer. I have to pull her off without dragging the whole lot with us. She only loosens her grip when I remind her of the delights of the cafe, in particular green frog marshmallow shortcakes. I regret this instantly. Now there's no chance of getting nutrition down her.

Later, at home, Grace and I have a go at digging over my new vegetable patch at the back of the garden. Bill, our next-door neighbour, comes out to trim his perfect hedge. I ask his advice about digging up the evil-looking fern sticking out of the back wall. Before I know it, he's grabbed his spade and set about the plant. Third warm glow of the day.

Tom rings tonight. Gracie tells him about her day. Bingo: warm glow number four.

Wednesday, 19 July 2000. We have received an invitation to a wedding from one of Tom's old acting friends who doesn't know about what has happened to Tom. He has asked me to send this reply:

Rehabilitation Ward,
Addenbrooke's Hospital,
Hills Road,
Cambridge
CB2 2QQ,

Friday, 14 July 2000

Dear Jackie,

I was so happy to receive the invitation to your wedding. It definitely touched a nerve, bringing back all those great memories of times gone by. Walthamstow, that bashed-up old Transit, Thelma in her hat, Freddie's 'Souvenirs' coat, Tina's cheesy chirpiness (*'Je m'appelle Marie...'*) and Nicky's wonderful fluent Franglais. And the year we spent in Paris, of course, which seems like a lifetime ago, but still flashes bright, black and white in the memory, in spite of all the rain, wine and daftness.

Things since then seem to have moved on so quickly, but looking back now, I remember those days as if they were a slow, carefree procession along streets and streets of light and laughter.

I literally can't remember when we last spoke or what news we shared. I only know it must have been a long time, since so much of my own life has spun around and, as it were, slid about on ice...

First of all, and at the heart of everything, there's Nic. She's very easy-going and caring and intuitively creative and attractive and pretty and attractive and clever and attractive and warm and full of smiles, and we just get on! We've been married for two years now, although we did know each other at Exeter in that other lifetime; in fact, I used to try to avoid her there because of the dangerous way she made me feel. Anyway, to cut a long story short, we managed to track each other down a few years ago and now we have two beautiful children: Grace, who's three, and Freddy (!), who's just turned seven months. We live in a tiny old cottage in a tiny old village on a peninsula in the middle of Rutland Water (literally, we're surrounded by it). Nic's a video director and conference producer, I help out with voiceovers, scripts, stuff and small children, and basically we just spend a whole lot of time enjoying life together. I think we're so grateful finally to have each other and to have this time together that life has become very, very simple and, with the children around us, full of love.

However. I've been very ill lately, which is why I'm writing to you from Addenbrooke's, in Cambridge. It's difficult to explain, but last December I contracted something called pneumococcal septicaemia (sepsis). It did quite a lot of damage very quickly, and unfortunately I had to have some serious amputations – both hands and both feet. Hard to believe and hard to understand and hard to accept. My face is also badly disfigured, so as well as learning to walk again, I have to stay here while they try to improve it – the next operation is on Monday, 17 July, when hopefully they'll be able to begin re-forming my nose. After that, I'm aiming to start going home for weekends – as you can imagine, I miss it all very much, especially little Grace, who I haven't seen for months.

The days here are full of physio and occupational therapy, where they help me to get used to the prosthetic arms and legs and to re-learn all the basic things like eating, washing, dressing and walking. Nic comes in nearly every day. Perhaps understandably we're even closer than ever, and although I sometimes feel desperate, right down deep inside I think I'm just as happy as I've ever been, knowing there's so much, soon, to return to. In the meantime, we're busy making and unmaking plans for the future: where we're going to live, how we're going to organise work, and, because we don't really know how soon I'll be mobile again, it's all quite fuzzy. Still, I'm determined to get back on my feet, even if they are made of plastic, and to find the way back home.

I've become so conscious of time passing – at the moment, it's like the ground falling away beneath us – and in future, I'm determined not to waste it. I think that means keeping life quite uncluttered and self-contained, and investing heavy amounts of time in the Nic-Grace-And-Freddy Bank, and in Tom Trying To Acquire Understanding.

Jackie, I hope you'll understand when I say that I don't think I'm going to be up to wedding celebrations, crowds and stuff by September. I've only been out three or four times in the car around Cambridge since last year, and at the moment, I feel dreadfully self-conscious about my appearance. I think for your planning purposes you'd best count us out, although if things improve quickly before then, I'll let you know.

Of course, I'd love to hear about what you're

up to and to know how you are. I'd pay a million pounds for a few hours and several bottles of wine with you, Tina and Freddie, and – weddings and operations aside – I hope we can all meet up on some other occasion in the not too distant future. As soon as I'm halfway fixed up in the face department, I'll be back in touch.

Naturally, we'll be thinking of you and Dave on 16 September – Nic, Grace, Freddy and I will all close our eyes at four o'clock and wish you both every happiness for the future.
With best wishes,
Tom

[Time passes so quickly. We didn't actually get to have that reunion with Jackie, Tina and Freddie until summer 2017. But we made it in the end, and these people remain precious friends. So much changes but the fun, friendship and laughter somehow remain. It's so important to keep close to the really important friends in your life.]

Monday 17th July 2000

The weirdest collection of days, barnacled with events. Sunday, we see a house, the perfect house. Within seconds of walking into the hallway I know this is right, and spend of the visit holding my breath in case we come across the bike repair business in the garden, or the raging damp, or the mad axe murderer next door. None of these, just a nasty seventies kitchen, and a half-done fireplace job. I can picture all of us here, a wish fulfilment maybe. The kids playing nicely in the light and airy rooms. Me wielding a spade, wiping the sweat from my brow, Tom, writing at the French windows. God, it's the start of a Stephen King movie! So an offer goes in, ten thousand less than the asking price. Then I spend half a day pen-chewing over a letter to our bank manager, a good mate from years gone by. It's not that we want more money, in fact we're looking at decimating the mortgage, but how will the bank view our new circumstances? This is Tom's territory. I fight a mild attack of vertigo and find I am actually enjoying organising our future.

Then we have Tom's surgery. Sunday, he is calm, but I see the signs of tension rising. He becomes more distant. By the time I leave we have had our statutory sob and I've reassured him a few hundred times that everything will be OK. But let's be realistic, Tom always feels shit, actually, after general anaesthetic. It seems all the despair of the last seven months engulfs him in those post-operative days, and I know I'll have to keep reinforcing how good things are in the face of his anger, disappointment and gloom. It is totally exhausting, and to be honest, I could quite happily engulf myself alongside him at these times.

Monday, we get a call from Tom. He is on the mobile, taking in the warm sunshine outside the Rosie Maternity

Hospital. Some lovely trees there. He is super-relaxed and sounds lovely. Grace talks to him. He tells her he hasn't been able to have any breakfast (Marmite on toast has become an addiction). She tells him about the boy who bit her at school. Tom must be totally mystified.

Monday, 24 July 2000

A week out on the wild side, after surgery last Monday afternoon. For most of the week afterwards, I've been trying to shake anaesthetic out of my ears and to scramble up out of bed – no physio, no exercise, no occupational therapy. In fact, for three days afterwards, no food or drink, since the operation left me with a fine set of stitches around my mouth. What they did was to de-bulk the surplus skin around the nose and mouth, also widening my mouth slightly; they'd also planned to insert transplanted bone tissue into my nose, but there was a delay in getting the right lines into me, so this was postponed. The surgeon took the stitches out this morning, and is seemingly quite happy with the results. But now he's off on two weeks' holiday and can't operate on the softer tissue anyway, so I have to wait another two or three weeks before I get another go.

So, progress... now I can scrunch my mouth open wider, and one or two people seem to think it looks a little less hideous. I've just about got my head together again after the anaesthetic, thanks in large part to the encouragement from Nic and Nina, who've spent long hours with me over the last few days. But they've gone now, it's five to nine in the evening, and I feel very, very alone. We've been talking about organising things for me to make my first home visit this weekend. It seems possible, so I'm obviously excited, but also a little taken aback. I'm nervous, because of Grace, and because of the things I still can't do independently. Still, four days to go, four days to practise, four days left to get back on my feet and to shake this fog from my head.

Nina spent a lot of time with me over the weekend, and it was very sad to say goodbye to her today, because if I do make it home every weekend now, it means that her visits to me at the hospital have come to an end. Dave, her husband, and Nina have alternated trips here throughout the last eight months, meaning that Nic can have a break and a day with Grace. We've all become closer as a result, and I can't quite put into words how grateful I've been for their love and support.

Tuesday, 25 July 2000. We have a friend called Mike, a charismatic 6ft 2in craftsman carpenter, with fair Marc Bolan hair and a girlish bubbliness. He built our kitchen, and has since gone on to be a kind of house-makeover TV celebrity. He played a song for us at our wedding cabaret entitled 'Dogface'. Some of the older relatives were bemused. It's the story of love across the ugliness barrier, with a

*rousing chorus of 'I love your Dogface'. Tom and I laughed
a lot at the time. Strange, because now, to be blunt, Tom
is a bit of a 'Dogface'. The shape and consistency of the
tissue around his nose and mouth have given him a slightly
droopy doggy look, like a special make-up job for a Disney
movie – 'half-man, half-pooch'. It's not scary, in fact it's
quite endearing. I predict he will be a big hit with small
children, given the reaction of the two-year-old who stood
and stared at him in Burger King yesterday.*

*More roller-coastering. The last bunch of surgery was
a success, although the surgeon didn't manage to put in
the bit of rib for the bridge of Tom's nose. Apparently
they'd spent so long putting in a central line, they didn't
want to risk rushing the slightly more risky bone harvest
(occasionally they can puncture a lung, I guess). Anyway
the result is still positive, and definitely less doggy. Tom's
nose is the right length now, and he has nostrils, albeit
slightly offline, and the size of Maltesers. They have
also widened his mouth opening, and put a skin graft
on the flat area beneath his nose. While his mouth still
resembles a small, slightly flattened ring doughnut, the
old Tom is slowly but surely starting to emerge through
the plasticine contours.*

*As predicted, after the surgery he did feel like shit. It
wasn't helped by the fact that a well-meaning nurse gave
him a 'Fortisip' through the stomach tube, just eighteen
hours after surgery. He promptly brought it all up,*

together with all the post-operative blood and muck. Then he panicked and refused to have anything apart from water for three days. So he got horribly dehydrated and hungry and as miserable as I've ever seen him. Then, the day he did start taking food, and just as his mood was lifting, he had a massive nosebleed, prompted, I think, by a bit of poking around and cleaning by Mr Malata. And of course it all coincided with a late-evening trip to Casualty for Grace when I got home. A possible ear infection, poor kid. She seems to have inherited Tom's tortuous ear canals!

Whatever, Tom is back to his old self now. Ward round with the consultant yesterday brought the best news possible: Tom can come home this weekend. Let me say that again: TOM CAN COME HOME THIS WEEKEND. More than that, his roll call of drugs is now down to low doses of penicillin, and hydrocortisone, together with a couple of vitamin supplements, skin cream, and polyfax ointment for the sutures on his face.

This afternoon I fell asleep reading Trevor Rees-Jones' book (the bodyguard who survived the crash that killed Princess Diana, Dodi Al Fayed and Henri Paul). The chapter on his stay in Intensive Care (or rather 'Re-animation') plunged me back to those early days. I remember, like a knife to the gut, the young doctor who told me Tom had gone into total organ failure, and the nurse who gave me his wedding ring, and his dressing gown, and Grace's orange blanket in a blue plastic hospital bag. I want to show them that drugs list. I realise I have been holding my breath for eight months. May I dare to exhale?

The dressing gown, by the way, hangs on our bedroom door. It hasn't been washed since December. It has a faint smell of Tom still. I used to hug it to my face to get close to him... to remember him as a warm presence next to me when he was so far away in every sense. I'm not sure what will happen to it now. My instinct is to get rid of it. Start afresh, as it were.

This morning the phone rings during the noisy wake-up hour. Grace is yelling 'I want a mousse!' over and over again. Freddy is bashing the buttons on a talking activity centre. It's an offer for the cottage – for the full guide price. In previous times this would have been so exciting. Now, it's another layer to add to the babble.

Wednesday, 26 July 2000

A drawn-out, tired day, after a semi-sleepless night. I'm nervous about going home after such a long time away, and especially of Grace's reaction when she sees my face, which still feels (and probably looks) twisted, tight and rudimentary. I ask myself, what's the worst thing that can happen? I suppose Grace might recoil in horror, screaming and shouting, and, after all these months of avoiding the mirrors, I will finally be faced with the full horror of what has happened to me. Rationalising, I tell myself that whatever happens, things between us can only get better – from first sight onwards. Surely, after a minute or two, the natural ties that bind us will begin to weave their web and then we'll be edging closer again? Or, at least, that's what I'm hoping. Perhaps if I looked in the mirror here, now, it would give me critical forward perspective on whatever reaction I get from Grace. Should I look? For the life of me, sitting here alone at 10pm, I don't want to cope with the distress of it – maybe tomorrow, where there are lifelines...

Ironically, in advance of my first weekend home, we have put our house up for sale. It's so tiny, even with little Freddy and Grace, we'll be bumping into each other like carts at the funfair – especially with my wheelchair. One plan is to buy a larger place with Nic's mum and all live together. Nic's already been to see an old red brick house in a nearby village, Braunston, in Rutland. By living together in this way, we'd be cutting our overheads quite considerably, so we'll see how it goes. I suspect the overall transaction may prove too complicated to sustain, and anyway, our thoughts may change after my first visit home. Who knows – I could prove to be a champion at getting up and down stairs on my bottom! Talking of which, I've been working with the occupational therapist again on independent toileting (imagine trying to do it all without hands), with some success – by the end of this week I need to have mastered it.

Lots of walking today. With Jan the Rehab

physiotherapist this morning, I used the gutter frame, sliding two or three times across the length of the gym; then this afternoon the other physio, Dave, supported me as I walked independently. It's very, very, very hard – you feel all the weight and tightness of the universe massing in the stumps underneath you – but I have to simply grin and bear it if I'm to make progress. I have more than enough reserves of sheer bloody-mindedness, but sometimes I feel as if the physical courage required is almost beyond me. Almost. I grit my teeth and shrink-wrap the pain, inching forward, thinking of my dear little family. *They need a man who walks, as well as talks*, I keep on thinking.

Dinner tonight on the terrace outside Rehab. Nic has brought me a delicious avocado and tomato salad, which I eat with the right-angled fork attachment on my artificial arms. Eating like this takes hours of patient persistence on both our parts, but we smile and talk and fumble our way forward, while Freddy, asleep in his pram, laughs and gurgles.

Tuesday, 1 August 2000. I'm worried. Tom's diary makes me sound like a mix of Julie Andrews and Delia Smith. He has clearly had too many drugs.

Tom did see his face at last. He took a long hard look while I had nipped off for Diet Cokes. I came back into his room to find him weeping silent tears, the paper towels ripped down around the washbasin mirror. I guess he decided that he should be able to face himself before putting Gracie through that test. I truly can't imagine how he feels, but once those tears and some of my own were dried, we discussed the issue no further. I haven't been able to see Tom as anything other than a face I love, even when he looked like a swollen aubergine. Now that he has made such huge progress, and I can see how remarkable the finished version will be, I sometimes find it difficult to think that others are seeing him for the first time, and to them he must look odd. More than that, until this moment Tom didn't really know how he looked. Whatever, Tom continues. His trips to the periphery of the outside world have continued. I guess you can call it putting on a brave face, literally, but there is no alternative if he wants to return to us, and he really doesn't look THAT bad.

The weekend. THE weekend. It's been and gone in a blur, all detail squashed flat by the sheer weight of the occasion. As planned, Grace and I go to rescue Tom on Friday afternoon. We are in borrowed car number two, my mum's little two-door Polo, borrowed car number one having blown up in a lightning storm on the A1 the night before. There's a story in its own right — smoke pouring into the passenger cabin from a melted head gasket, me grabbing Freddy from his kiddie seat in the back, fingers fumbling for the clips on his harness, lashing rain, and an unlikely white knight in the Shell garage at Thornhaugh.

Anyway, Friday. Things aren't looking too promising for our domestic reunion. It is hot. Grace is sweltering and whimpering in the back seat. She is grumpy from lack of sleep and earache. I, meanwhile, am sweating cobs, the sun thumping in through the window, which I can only open a couple of inches. I wonder if Sergio Leone ever considered the A14 as a location. We stop in a suburb of Cambridge for Calpol, drinks and Love Hearts. Grace demands to have a wee beside a tree in the chemist's car park. Suddenly she is a different child. I can't tell if it's the bladder relief, the drugs or the sugar, but someone has smiled down on us, and we trundle on. My heart is thumping as we trail up the corridor. Gracie is holding my hand. She has the sticky pack of Love Hearts in the other, the message on the topmost, well-fingered sweet for Daddy, 'My Guy'. It's all her own idea. At first she hangs back as we approach his room. Then she darts into a chair, hands over her face. For a few moments she sits, taking sneaky peeks at him through gaps between her fingers. Tom and I chat as I put clothes and medicines in a bag; we are prepared for this. Her attitude screams curiosity. Gotcha, girlie! Thank you, Marion.

Half an hour later we have made the tortuous trip through the corridors of Addenbrooke's. Gracie has spotted a game, Frustration, in the room. She asks her dad if she can take it. The box is quite big but somehow she struggles with it down the long corridors towards the Rosie Maternity Hospital. Tom and Grace wait while I get the car. By the time I come back they are chatting animatedly about the relative merits of Chicken Nuggets and Coca-Cola. I fight an urge to break into 'I'd like to Teach the World to Sing'.

The heat hasn't abated, but somehow the journey home seems quicker and cooler. As we make the descent alongside Rutland Water I can see Tom taking it all in. I ask if he remembers all this. He looks at me, eyes articulate... how could anyone forget? As I had half-guessed, Tom decides that he is going to walk up the front path. This is verging on scary. I trust him not to fall – this is a performance after all, and he would never take to the stage without knowing all his moves, all his lines. Our progress is surprisingly fast. He's a very fluent walker, but when we reach the steps I ask him if he has practised these. 'Um... I don't think so.' I yell for the kids' nanny, Suzanne. She's 6ft in heels, Tom and I a good half-foot smaller. Still, we make solid, if lopsided props, and in a few moments Tom's in the living room, sitting on the settee he left so unceremoniously nine months ago. The moment is indescribable. Now I notice how tiny Tom looks. He sits, gazing benevolently, guzzling in the detail, the textures, the colours...

Weekends are odd anyway. No Suzanne. Two kids. My own compulsion to do everything, but in as casual a manner as possible. Then to add Tom back into the equation. As usual we try to do too much. Saturday morning: the *kids make sure I am up before I am in danger of having anything like enough sleep. I have already fed Freddy at 4am, and moved him and me into the spare bed at 6.30 to avoid disturbing Tom. Thankfully, by the time Tom surfaces, we have eaten, bathed, and had our first three tantrums (Grace two, me one).*

I take him a cocktail of multi-vitamins and orange juice, plus penicillin. He wants to make his own way from room to room. This involves equal measures of sweat and swearing, 'Oh God!' as he tries to get up from a low seat. We also have to do an elegant tango to execute the bathroom routine. He has a commode chair, which is slightly bigger than the available floor space in the bathroom. 'Oh bugger!' — I drop a bag of drugs and ointments into the bath.

I have arranged to drop Gracie off with her friend Lucy. This means us all getting out of the house by 11.45. By 11.30 Tom is sitting eating a pile of Marmite on toast fingers, and he hasn't had the long promised bath yet. He is struggling, quietly. I have buttered the toast while it is too hot, and the fingers droop from his fork like wilted leaves. Freddy eyes him up and is starting to look suspiciously hungry again. I realise I have as much chance of getting out of the house as winning the lottery two weeks running. I ring Anna, Lucy's mum. She is her normal laid-back self. We have as much time as we need — that probably still isn't enough.

Stress has no place in our home. I decided that on 10 December. The trick, I realise, is to be more continental in our attitude to time. Secretly I always fancied being Italian, and Tom's driving has always been 'Latin' to put it politely. Besides, they also have the best food, cars and clothes.

Sunday, we are all good Italians. Tom sleeps till nearly 11, but I suspect he didn't nod off till 4am. Last night when I came up to bed I found him lying alongside the cot where Freddy was sleeping. It was then that I felt a huge guilty pang that Tom has been denied these simple pleasures of parenthood. Today there is nothing more pressing on the agenda than a haircut for Tom. His hair grows fast and upright as cress on cotton wool. Unfortunately I can't find the right scissors or comb, and I worry about getting hairs down the felt trachy collar. Also, Grace has decided to make sand birthday cakes for us all. She wanders into the kitchen dripping sand from every crevice, asking for suspiciously large amounts of water. At this point I would normally have called the emergency service – Mum – to take the pressure off. Unfortunately we have her car, and the prospect of getting the whole circus together to make the journey to pick her up is just too much. I can't remember the Italian national anthem, so I hum 'Ritornere a Sorrento' instead. It helps, I think.

The weekend has been amazing. It is just dreadful

to think of going back to Cambridge. We drag things out to the last moment, but by 7.30 we have to face the inevitable. Tom takes one heroic walk back up the garden and suddenly the time's passed. The only consolation: the next weekend and, we hope, good news about his permanent return.

HAMBLETON

8 August 2000

I am determined to walk down my own front path to greet my daughter. Things between us have been so difficult. She is only three years old, and by the time I am discharged, I have not seen her for nine months. That's twenty-eight weeks, one hundred and ninety-six days, four thousand seven hundred and four hours, two hundred and eighty two thousand two hundred and forty seconds. This is the little girl I'd given up my job for, and looked after as a full-time dad. So it seems only fitting that she should see me walk up the gravel path to the house, unassisted. I don't want to be pushed, delivered like some parcel, some *thing*. Hence all that time in the gym, all those hours on the rowing machine, building up strength, increasing my resistance to pain.

They give me a walking frame to take home with me. At first, I'm appalled. The idea of a thirty-nine-year-old man having to use such a thing is ludicrous. But I do, absolutely need it. I lean very heavily on it. There are times, early on, when the pain of every step is excruciating. It makes me cry out, it makes me swear. But you just have to go on: you just have to, if you want to walk.

I am home – in my own front room. The last time I was in that room was last December, an expectant time in every way: two birthdays, Christmas, a Millennium and the birth of my second child.

Grace has made a 'Welcome Home' card for me; she has flowers – 'I got a video, do you want to watch it with me?' Watching videos together was always our thing, from when she was a baby.

I've been waiting for nine months to see my girl. She wouldn't come to hospital because she was frightened of my face, and all I could do was to think of her, write her notes; send her gifts. All that time has gone. I'm so different, and she's grown from being two to being three. But now we are back together, and once again I'm surely the luckiest man in the world. But...

I don't know how I'm going to get up the stairs. I don't know how I am ever going to open a letter. I don't know if I will ever work again. I don't know if I will be able to pay any bills. I don't know where I left my chequebook.

I don't know how painful it will be when they take my tracheostomy out. I don't know if Grace will ever get used to the deformed way I look. I don't know how I'm going to go to the toilet. I don't know how I'm going to wash. I don't know how I'm going to brush my teeth. I don't know how I'm going to hold a telephone. I don't know how I'm going to eat. I don't know how I'm going to get my clothes on, or take them off. I don't know how I'm going to look into a mirror. I don't know how I'm going to walk into a room full of strangers. I don't know how I'm going to walk. I don't know how I am going to hug anyone, ever again. I don't know if I can ever breathe through my nose again. I don't know if will ever have lips again.

I don't know why any of this happened. Or if I can ever kiss Nic again.

I think of the last time I ever did any of these things, with my old hands and feet. It seems wrong that I can't remember the exact time, the exact moment, the precise action. It seems crazy that something like this could happen to a healthy adult, with absolutely no hint or suggestion of a symptom. It's just all gone, and I can't remember, and I don't know why.

I try to cling to the important things that I have left. My family, of course, and this enchanting, beautiful cottage that we live in. If I can hold on to those things, that will be an achievement.

Sunday, 3 September 2000

Time is moving so quickly now. I've hardly had the chance to turn around, and it's September. We're looking up, looking ahead with a growing sense of expectation, allowing the days to develop their own pattern. Sometimes we're systematic and organised, sometimes it's like being in a maze and we just trust to luck that we're taking all the right turns. Getting things done is like trying to rationalise a conversation with Grace: you have to take three shots at it, bending your back into the effort, forcing the pace; twisting the direction.

My left knee has been weak for a few days so I've been taking ibuprofen and resting it. We did travel into Leicester on Thursday to see the physio and prosthetist: lots of talking and a little practice going up and down stairs ('good leg to heaven, bad leg to hell'), plus they re-lined one of my leg inserts to make it slightly more comfortable. On Friday I saw Mr Malata, the plastic surgeon, at Peterborough Hospital. He's making arrangements to remove the peg tube from my stomach and to cap off the tracheostomy device that protrudes from my throat. Then more surgery, in a couple of months.

Life at home has a strange quality. Time with Nic is my most precious possession. We're like superheroes together. I don't need anything else — all the beauty of life is there. But the everyday practicalities are awkward, painful, frustrating; we tread a path around them together, conscious we must just keep things together. There are times when I can barely contain my frustration. I'd like to do so much more for Nic, for the children and for myself, and I feel very depressed. It can be agonising: having to wait for help to get up in the morning, or to eat breakfast, sitting in a room with Freddy crying, unable to move or to help him... We've paid a deposit on a new house down in Oakham. It's totally different: an en suite and a bathroom, modern, and much cheaper than our cramped little cottage. But our buyers have pulled out. Post Office cotttage is tiny and full of character, but it's a challenging purchase in some ways – unique. There are a hundred reasons why a buyer might get cold feet. So the *For Sale* board is back up and we'll have to wait and see what happens.

The trees are thick with the summer, the church sleeps on, the sky slides over it and, for minutes at a time as I stare from the window, stops. Hambleton is quiet and empty, a prison village for the wealthy and the disconnected. The signpost on the green outside our window says 'No Through Road' in three different directions. I suppose there will always be days like these: Sundays for the soul.

STARFISH

Monday, 4 September 2000

To Leicester again for another long session at the Disablement Services Centre. They're going to make new arms (at last), as what's left of the muscles in my upper arms apparently still gives out enough 'myoelectric' power to move prosthetic hands. We've also asked them to adapt my false legs so that I can put them on myself and rejoin the human race for breakfast in the morning – without having to wait, and wait, and wait.

My short-term memory is still shot to pieces. I was at the hospital for nearly four hours today and yet I can barely remember what we talked about. I suppose it's the continuing effect of the drugs and lingering anaesthetic. Cutlery... That's another thing we talked about – using proper cutlery instead of the bent right-angled variety that bolt into the ends of my arms. And... Oh, I don't know where the conversation drifted; for all I know time stood still on its three awkward corners – fate, hope and serendipity – and we sat for half-hours at a time in suspended animation.

The green hills and the giant white clouds stood still as we raced by and back to Hambleton-by-Haystack. Grace has been to nursery school for the first day of a new term and is completely exhausted; Freddy is starting to crawl and drag himself from room to room, leaving me behind, rooted to the spot. He's small and friendly, full of laughter and smiles: the perfect ally, in fact, rolling

220

over and over for just the sheer fun of it. If you were an alien newly arrived from Outer Space and needed a guide to the world, I can think of no better partner.

Tuesday, 26 November 2000

For some reason, it has been weeks since I wrote this diary. I suppose we have been busy trying to develop a routine, but there's also a sense in which I have been trying to distance myself from this whole experience of being away in hospital, and ill, and everything having been broken up into so many pieces. In some ways, the diary ties me down to the hospital bed of bad experiences, so I have neglected it, wilfully.

So, what of September, what of October? Well, the weeks have passed quickly. There have been plenty of appointments at Leicester General Hospital and at the smaller hospital down in Oakham for limb-fitting, physiotherapy and occupational therapy. As ever, progress has been slow and for some reason my left knee gave way, so I couldn't walk. This has limited life greatly, restricting me to the house and to the wheelchair. I saw a specialist consultant about it. He wanted to put a camera inside the joint to see what's wrong, but they've deferred this until the next operation, which itself was put back a month to 4 January as a result of the NHS winter cutbacks.

We've had plenty of visitors, and at the moment my brother Adam is over from Australia. Adam is possibly the most positive person in the world, so it's great having him around – just what I need. He has a knack of looking past difficulty, and finding the comedy way forward. As soon as I came out of my coma, he was sending me the thumbs up in every message. Right to this day whenever I'm faced with a huge challenge I can hear his voice in my head – 'Come on, Tom – you can do it...' We have been out for a few drinks down in Oakham and at the pub across the road in the village. This is great, as it makes me feel part of normal life again, although it's always a struggle to get in and out of these places and I feel very self-conscious. I hide in the corner underneath the brim of my cap, like some fugitive, or rock star.

It's cold. Winter is coming quickly. We are all slowly getting a little stronger. Predictably, we have become so attached to the house again that we've put aside thoughts of moving down to Oakham for the time being. It's so cosy and familiar here, so much part of who and what we are, that it seems too great a sacrifice to give it up, just for the sake of a little extra space. Still, we will have to think again, looking at the state of our finances. I often wish I could quickly re-establish some kind of regular income, just enough to cover the mortgage, our living expenses and a little extra to build out the kitchen at the back of the house, and I suppose this will come in time – at least, that's what everyone tells me. But I'm impatient. I just want to get on and get things fixed, so we can start living and enjoying the rest of our lives.

Freddy is restless at night and Nic doesn't get enough sleep, even though once or twice a week Grace goes down to Nic's mum's house to stay, just to make things a little easier. Anyway, he's a beautiful boy, quick to smile, like his mother, and full of joy at the prospect of walking, cuddles and toast. Grace, as ever, is a whirlwind, and we can hardly keep up with her. School in the morning uses up some of her energy, but the rest of the day is a bit of a battle; I'm not sure that the world will ever be big enough for her. Or perhaps it's my understanding that's not deep enough, and perhaps my expectations are too high — it takes a lot of energy to engage with her. I don't try hard enough, or when I do, my concentration falters after a minute or two. She sleeps soundly at night, exhausted, while Nic wrestles with Freddy and I lie still, thinking about all this.

✶

I try to make sense of the world in the New Millennium. The mood of things has definitely changed. I notice an overwhelming superficiality. *Who Wants To Be A Millionaire?* dominates the TV. All the cars on the road seem flimsy and new (X-reg already?). The news seems crazy and chaotic, what with floods, train crashes and the amazing, farcical Bush/Gore American election result. The expression on the newsreader's face seems more perplexed every day, and everything seems to be about money, fame and misfortune. A footballer meets a Spice Girl and the rest is silence, except for the whisper of the cash being counted in the background. Meanwhile, ordinary people struggle to understand and to get through the day, to pay the bills and get online. And when they do, they find they are missing nothing. Time itself seems to slip much more quickly through our fingers. A whole nation is driving at high speed down the A1, looking for the next traffic jam, for the next hamburger stopover, appreciating nothing except the velocity and greed. Real thinkers, and those who represented older values – such as Scottish First Minister Donald Dewar, who recently died – are pulled over by the thought police of the new order and told to stop thinking. We cling only to the surface of things: the catalogue, the website, the share price.

I know I am a millionaire because of the time I have left and because of the people I have around me. Looking into the faces of the ones I love, I catch reflections of heaven and immortality – when my eyes are open.

I am in a wheelchair most of the time, but it's the most impractical thing in the world. Inside a small country cottage with just four small rooms including the bathroom and only toilet on the ground floor, it's a bit of a nightmare. It's a job just to get the thing through the narrow wooden doorways, and I am constantly catching the jambs as I try to squeeze through, taking splinters and lumps out of them. Getting upstairs and downstairs is just impossible. Nic has to physically push me up the stairs at night and I hover precariously on each step. It's humiliating, exhausting, strange and intimate, all at the same time. It's the kind of activity that can only bring us even closer together, but it's quite an experience.

It soon becomes obvious that I'm going to have to get on my feet again — that is, to start using my artificial legs. It's quite evident to Nic and to me that there's not much future for a grown man who has to be carried everywhere. I've got plastic legs in an enormous NHS bag in the wardrobe, so I put them on. Walking in them is excruciating. The plastic casing is hard and it pinches the skin of my leg stumps so painfully — even three steps brings tears to my eyes. There is also an abscess eating a hole into the bone of my left knee. I have it dressed by the district nurse every two days, but there is seemingly little prospect of it healing over anytime soon. However, I have no option: I have a wife and two children to support. Either I learn to walk and triumph over this disability, or I sit like a vegetable in a wheelchair for the rest of my life.

I close my eyes. Nothing will stop me. I walk forward.

Soon enough I am stepping out of the front door and taking short walks down the peninsular road. And when I say short walks, I mean *short*. At the start, it's just twenty steps, then the next day, twenty-five. Day in, day out, I just add another five steps, then I find I can make it all the way to the red Royal Mail post box. This gives me the idea that every day I could take a letter and mail it, so I begin to do that. I write to my mother, my sister and my brother, letting them know how we're doing at home, making these daily improvements, and how much their support has meant to me.

It snows. Early, laying snow, thick on the ground, making everything picture postcard, white, sparkling and startling. I continue my routine, my hundred yards every day, in all weathers – even snow. With my new prosthetic legs, slumped against my 'old man' frame, I inch my way through the snow, along the village road. A strange, hunched figure, shuffling along, pausing between every step. Snow is coming down, swirling all around me.

As soon as the weather clears, we get into a routine of going down to the edge of Rutland Water to sit in the afternoon sun. Freddy is wrapped up warmly in a blanket, and we can see his face peeping out from under the hood of his pram.

Nic pushes him slowly up and down the waterside path, while Grace and I sit watching from a bench, in front of the Old Hall, a building that looks like it is half in and half out of the Water. Grace is playing with her woollen Womble doll, making it sit up against the back of the wooden bench, animating it. I've been telling her about a story I'm going to write, when I can get down to it.

'And are there any Wombles in it?'

We have zero income. Nic is wholly occupied, for what seems like the foreseeable future, with looking after the children – but also with caring for me, potentially forever. It's beginning to set off alarm bells in my head – and I've only been home from hospital for a few months.

Money initially hasn't been a huge issue for us – Nic has earned well for the last few years and we've built up a healthy bank balance. But it's fast being used up since she had to stop working just before I got ill in December 1999. Now, nearly a year on, with a big mortgage and two small people to care for, over the next few months things will get eye-wateringly tight. There's no way we're going to be able to pay for adaptions to the quaint but hopelessly impractical bathroom, or child-minding, or anything that might give Nic a break from the demands of constant caring, let alone the mortgage and the bills.

Nic reminds me of the sponsored bike race our friends did to raise money while I was in Addenbrooke's: twenty-one miles round Rutland Water. Nic, Freddy in his buggy, and Grace stood on the small green outside our cottage, waving off the assembled horde, dressed in various states of sensible athletic gear and pantomime outfits. These were people she hadn't seen for months; she hadn't spoken to them herself. Yet the response was incredible.

'OK – let's get this show on the road. THREE... TWO... ONE...'

She swiftly passed the megaphone to Grace: 'GET READY, SET, GO!!!'

The cyclists waved at her, charged off down the dirt track and disappeared into the trees.

There are other fundraising events. Nic has to attend them all, swapping her jeans and T-shirts for formal evening gear. One minute she's bathing my leg stump wounds and fixing the wiring on a prosthetic hand, the next she's nursing Freddy to sleep and drawing a pirate face on Grace in preparation for a party; then she has to dig to the back of her wardrobe to find her one smart outfit and attend a formal dinner, three and a half hours' drive away at Watford Golf Club. There's a dinner and auction event in aid of the trust fund that's been set up for me. A hundred and fifty people sit in evening dress at tables for ten. There are bottles of champagne, the meal is superb, there is a string quartet... The staff, all in formal dress, dart about, waiting at tables. Outside, it's dark, cold, windy and rainy, but inside the dinner hall, the place is buzzing. Nic sits at the top table, looking pale and a little awkward.

It's the first time in ages that she's been at any kind of social event – let alone one where she is the focus of public attention. She hardly knows or recognises anyone; she has to make a speech. It's a strange experience for her – being suddenly so far away from home, away from the cottage, away from the family. Addressing a large group of strangers, reading from cue cards, presenting the detail of her most private tragedy. Trying not to make it alarm her audience because there's always some detail that makes people recoil from the gritty reality of our strange story, when she's forced to recount it. They listen carefully; the mood is serious, some of the diners (including the men) are tearful.

It makes me angry that my wife has to stand up and say all these things out loud: we are just as proud of our independence and our ability to look after ourselves as anyone else. In any normal situation, I would have done anything to protect her from having to do this, but this is no normal situation.

This is what she says:

'I would have assumed that as we live in a so-called caring society, where billions of pounds are spent annually on health, there would be sophisticated systems in place that would protect victims of this kind of illness and their

families at their critical time of need. I wouldn't have blamed anyone for assuming that. But the truth is that it just isn't so.

If Tom was a serviceman who had been injured in the line of duty, if he'd been injured playing sport or in some kind of industrial accident, then yes, there would have been systems and insurance policies and organisations in place to help us.

But Tom didn't wear a uniform, he never picked up a gun and he never did anything to put himself or us at risk. He was just Mr Normal, going about his daily business, looking after his baby daughter while I went out to earn our living.'

I don't go with her. To me it just doesn't seem right, to sit there and have all these people talking about me, and – however good their intentions – staring at me. Instead, for the first time since I've been home from hospital, I'm left alone in the cottage. Nic's mum has stepped in and volunteered to look after Grace and Freddy, so I try and occupy myself and stay out of trouble.

There is football on the TV. England are playing Greece and that kid David Beckham is lining up a long free-kick. Just as he approaches the ball to kick it, the TV remote falls from my knee to the floor and the screen goes blank. The remote clatters onto the wooden floor and disappears under the sofa. *Damn! I bet he's scored as well – right in the top corner of the goal, I just bet he has.* I can't reach the remote – I can't even get off the sofa to go for a pee – so for the rest of the night, I just sit there.

A hundred and fifty miles away, Nic is still on her feet...

'*His illness came out of nowhere. And since there is no legislation written for freak disasters that come out of nowhere to strike down Mr Normal, there is absolutely no safety net that supports him – or his family. There is nothing to help us confront the challenges we are going to have to face in the next ten, twenty or even fifty years. As far as the State is concerned, all they have to do is to provide him with two sticks to stand on and a steel hook to do everything else with – then their obligations to us are totally discharged. So, if you can find it in your hearts to help us do a little better than that – help us to fund the new technology that will make Tom's life a better, more bearable one – and enable him to regain his self-respect and allow him to make the contribution he's still capable of – then, as well as being more caring than the society you live in, you will have the undying gratitude of a small but determined family from Rutland.*

'*Finally, for obvious reasons, I'm afraid Tom couldn't make it here tonight. I know he would have been extremely interested to meet you all, although as a proud bloke from Essex, he'd be as embarrassed as hell, and probably wouldn't know quite what to say — for once. But I will be sure to give him your very best wishes when I get home. I will have to carry him up the stairs to bed, as I do every night, but when I do that, I'll be sure to let him know that he has a hundred and fifty new friends who are keen to support us. That will mean the world to him.*

Thank you.'

As one, the dinner guests rise and give her a standing ovation.

It's 2am when Nic comes home. I'm still on the sofa, with the lights on in the living room. The TV screen is just snow. When I ask her how it went down in Watford, she just raises her eyebrows and smiles:

'That was *weird*.'

She rolls up he sleeves of her smart jacket and gets ready to help shove me physically up the stairs to bed.

'No, *this* is weird.'

* * *

In the long, thin back kitchen at Post Office Cottage, I'm about to test my new robotic arms. *Myoelectric*, they call them, because they have sensors inside the stump casing and when you flex your muscles against them, they rotate the hand at the wrist, or open and close the hand itself, so you can grip stuff.

Nic, Freddy and Grace are sitting at the table with me,

waiting nervously for me to try the arms and to see if they will actually work.

In front of me on the table is a big washing-up bowl. Inside the bowl, in the middle, is a mug with a straw in it. I look round at the faces of my family then down at the mug before taking a deep breath. They watch expectantly as I stretch out my right arm and reach into the bowl. I focus hard with my eyes on the handle of the mug and squeeze the outer muscle on the lower part of my right arm, just below the elbow.

Whirr. Bzzzz. Movement.

The four plastic fingers of the electric hand close slowly towards the thumb. They tighten firmly against the fat china handle of the mug – so firmly that I can confidently lift it from the bowl. When I see the tip of the straw approaching my mouth, I can hardly believe it. The mug itself feels very heavy, but with a little effort and a lot of concentration I can manage to hold it in situ just below by mouth.

It's a triumph. I lower my head again to take another sip.

Then, just as I am on the point of sucking up more tea, Grace's eyes grow wide with horror as the hand that is holding the mug starts to rotate again *involuntarily*. Whatever I do – whichever muscle I twitch inside the casing of the arm – I am incapable of stopping the hand swivelling away from me and tipping its contents not into the bowl but down the cream-coloured kitchen. The hand, still clutching the mug tightly, continues to go round and round in circles.

I look at the others. Grace is holding her breath. Nic is biting her lip and is trying so hard not to laugh that she is shaking. She fails to hold it in, and starts giggling loudly. So does Grace.

'It's OK,' I say, 'I guess it's going to take a while before I get the hang of this. Rome wasn't built in a day. But you get the idea?'

Crying and laughing – but mostly laughing – Nic nods at me. This is not the last time this will happen. In fact, the brown tea stain will be joined by many more, including a dramatic Jackson Pollock-style splosh from an entire bottle of red wine, when my hand freezes completely, upside-down.

The first set of arms was the end product of a year-long process of negotiation, consultation, measuring, re-measuring, casting, fitting, re-fitting, testing and training on the part of the Leicester Disablement Services (DSC) team, including a genius prosthetist, Allan, and an occupational therapist who argued my case with the NHS for two myoelectric arms (they only wanted to give Tom one, in case he didn't take to it). We owe them a huge debt of gratitude. They must have seen how hard Tom was prepared to work to be a functioning part of our family. The cost of the arms, especially the maintenance involved, would have been prohibitive, despite the heroic fundraising efforts of friends.

I walk to the bench outside the church: forty steps. The sun on my face and on my neck feels warm and comforting. After half a year inside a hospital under artificial light it feels like a gift from God. I examine my new arms, turning them over and over, staring at them. I rotate my right hand; I open and close it. A summer breeze stirs the leaves in the tree above me. I look up. A leaf falls. I reach out and let it drop into the open palm of my false right hand. I close it on the leaf – I can do that. This is freedom. It means I have a viable future, and that the people who said I was finished were wrong. It makes me happy.

We've had to argue long and hard to get the funding from our health authority for the new myoelectric hands, but ever since I've had them, life has been easier. Already I have learned to do some basic things for myself now. I can even feed myself a little, and do up my own trousers after I've been to the bathroom. I'm clawing back some of the skills I lost; I'm fighting back.

Evening. For the hundredth time, Grace and I are watching the Disney video *Robin Hood: Prince of Thieves* and whistling along with the theme tune. We're big fans of the Sheriff of Nottingham, who in this cartoon is a wily old cat voiced by the great Peter Ustinov. We watch this film over and over, as well as *Baby Mozart*, which I'm hoping will turn Grace into a genius, as it's too late for me. Grace is also drawing. She calls her mum into the room from the kitchen:

'Mum, how do you draw a cow?'

Nic replies as she returns to the kitchen. She has our latest bank statements out on the table and is trying to do sums with a pencil and a calculator.

'Well, you start with a sort of squashed circle for the body, then a smaller one for the head, then add two horns, the tail, then the legs.'

'My cow isn't going to have any legs.'

There's a silence, then Nic reappears, nervously, in the doorway.

'Why?'

Grace looks up and stares at the video for a moment, then absent-mindedly says:

'Because they know it's going to rain and they're all lying down, of course.'

I look at Nic.

'Oh,' she says, relieved.

★

There are daily visits from the Rutland District Nurses, who are jolly, old-fashioned and fastidious. I have wounds on my legs that will seemingly never heal and require regular dressing, and the plastic stent tubes in my 'nose' need to be removed, cleaned and reinserted every day. It is a painful and traumatic experience.

Pain has become an everyday currency for me – different degrees of it. There's the small, pinching pain I get when Nic first puts my legs on in the bedroom and I have to walk down the stairs to the bathroom. Then there's the deeper, more enduring pain that I feel on the end of my arm stump, trying to carry the weight of my artificial limbs. There's exposed bone at the end of my right arm and the weight of the hand I carry is considerable there: it grates. Most alarming of all is the 'phantom' pain I get, usually at night, when a muscle somewhere in my leg stump starts to twitch. This recurs every two minutes, hour upon hour. It's as if someone is sticking a dagger very slowly up through the leg stump, then twisting it. It makes me want to die.

The nurses help as much as they can, but it's Nic, inevitably, who does 99 per cent of the caring. All day, she's fetching something for me, making this or that better, covering my raw wounds with plaster and making endless visits and repeated emergency requests down at the pharmacy, ordering and re-ordering my list of medications, bringing them home to sort them out, and dispensing them. She washes me like a baby in the bath, feeds me, spoonful after spoonful, cutting up my food so that it'll go through the pinhole of my distorted, grafted mouth.

No matter how frugal we are, stalking the market for end-of-day bargains, buying our clothes at Oxfam, there's always the bottomless pit of direct debits. The biggest expense is the mortgage, which is swallowing up our savings. And while we have savings, there's no question of being eligible for anything more than the Disabled Living Allowance (DLA), which in turn is being obliterated by the cost of petrol to hospital appointments in Cambridge, Leicester or Peterborough. It's a vicious cycle.

So here I am, back at Hambleton, poring over the bank statement again. Freddy's in his white plastic high chair, out in the kitchen, banging a spoon and a baby dish around. Grace's colouring things are on the table by the back wall where she was sitting earlier. She's drawn a picture of me with ruby red lips, yellow hair and a Lego nose and written underneath it: MY DADDY IS A ROBOT!!! Radio 4 is babbling away in the background, darkness claws at the windows, and a family of foxes runs round the garden.

I can't think what's going to happen. I don't even know if we could get another mortgage, given that Nic's shut her business down and I'm not working long-term. Maybe we'll have to rent somewhere, in some other place. It will be sad to leave Rutland and go back to a town or a city, but our options are narrowing by the day.

In all this, we forget to be happy. We're too busy

minding kids, attending appointments, and fretting about the future.

✦

I'm wedged tight halfway up the stairwell, like a very damaged Spider-Man. I've got both my elbows high up behind my back, squeezed into the corners of the stair above me, and both my knees splayed to each side, trying to get some purchase on the walls. That's not easy without feet or fingers. There's a strong danger of losing my hold and slipping down stairs on my backside. Nic is doing what she can to help, but she's distracted by dangerous noises from the kitchen. She's not sure what's happening down there. I tell her to go: I'll just have to hold myself here. But she knows that if she moves, she could bring my full weight piling down on top of her; or I could seriously injure myself on the hard plaster of the walls, or the tiled floor at the bottom.

'MUMMMM-EEEEEE!'

'I'm coming, darling.' Nic starts off back down the stairs, but before she can reach the bottom, Grace appears holding the jagged half of a smashed cereal bowl. Nic and I stare down at her.

'Grace, just listen to me. Very, very carefully. Now I want you to put the bowl down ever so slowly on the floor in front of you. Can you do that for me please?'

'Bowl... down... on... floor?'

'Yes, that's right. But in front of you, where you can see it, not behind you. Do you understand?'

Grace takes her thumb out of her mouth, stares at me for a second, then at her mum. Her brow furrows deeply. All of a sudden she lifts the broken bowl high above her head, then throws it as hard as she can onto the quarry tile floor. *Kerrrrasssssshhhhhhh!* The sound is terrifying. There is a hailstorm of flying china, vicious splinters of slate and sharp wood as the stoneware ricochets against the back of the front door.

Nights are disturbed. We don't have an upstairs bathroom, and there is no way I can make it up and down those stairs in an emergency. So I'm reduced to peeing into one of the cardboard bottles the district nurse has given us. If the bottle is within reach, I can just about grab it with the stumps of my arms and, sitting on the edge of my bed, I can position it where it needs to be. But doing this in the dark is just asking for trouble, so first I have to wake Nic, so that she can turn on the light. If I'm in a hurry to go, rousing her from her well-earned rest can take just a moment too long. So naturally, I try to hold it whenever I can, because the last thing I want to do is to disturb her. I have to lie for hours like that.

We also have Freddy asleep in his cot, in the corner of our bedroom. Any of this night-time activity is likely to wake him. He starts crying and wants to get into bed with Nic. And that means Nic is awake for the rest of the night.

Nic is in the eye of the storm, and it's getting worse with every day that passes. There's pressure from every direction. Pressure from me, trying to cope with the practical and psychological impact of my disability. Pressure from the children, who are naturally extremely demanding, every hour of the day. Pressure from the bank, as our financial resources disappear like sand through an hourglass. Pressure from her mother, who visits daily and is obviously concerned at my fluctuating state of mind and the demands on Nic as a carer. She wants everything to be right for her daughter, and why shouldn't she?

Nic's in the back kitchen, with her mum, talking about it.

'What do you mean, he doesn't want to move?'

Nic shakes her head. Grace comes out of the sitting room dragging her coat. With one thumb jammed firmly in her mouth, she squeezes past my wheelchair and Nic, then stomps off down the front path, calling out to her.

'Put your coat on!'

Grace ignores her and gets into Jean's car.

'This isn't healthy, Nicola.'

Nic shrugs. 'What can I do?'

'Talk to him, explain how worried you are. Make a new start, all of us. You've got to start thinking about yourself – and Grace and Freddy.'

When Jean has left, Nic opens the dreaded purple box file, takes out a bank statement, and slides it across the table.

'Things aren't good.'

We don't have to look at the balance. I know it, right down to the last penny, but I study the sheet of paper out of courtesy. There's a long silence between us. *Why am I pretending to resist? Why cause so much trouble, when things are difficult enough as they are?*

I'm just so angry; I'm kicking up rough, like a difficult teenager. I hate having to let things go. I hate feeling that something is being taken away. When Nic and I discuss selling Post Office Cottage, we're not talking about bricks and mortar. It's as if the surgeons are coming back at me, and want to perform another amputation. They've already taken both my arms, both my legs, my lips, my nose, those bits of my face – and now they want my soul.

I try for the thousandth time to work out some way we could hold on to the cottage. Surely, in this age of easy credit and relaxed lending, we could find some more reasonable repayment schedule? But our finances are so weak now – we can't contemplate approaching lenders with no income. It's hopeless. We just have to accept what's coming to us, downsize and get on with it.

My mind skitters back to when I was ten years old. I'm in the house in Eastwood, Essex, where my father left us to seek fame and fortune in London. Two workmen are nailing boards over the windows of our house. I'm wearing my school uniform even though my mum told me not to, and I'm standing at the end of my front path in case any of my mates come past. Mum told me not to say anything at school because she's sold the house without telling my dad and she's afraid he'll come after her for the money. I see my sweetheart from up the road walk past on the other side of the street. She calls out to me, but I can't go over.

This is the last time I will ever see any of my friends.

The front door opens and my mum comes out with my brother and sister. They are each carrying a suitcase but they are struggling. The workmen stop what they're doing out of respect. It's heartbreaking and undignified, like the retreat from Dunkirk. My mum is crying openly. She reaches out with her free hand to take mine, and we walk away from our house.

Ten yards further on, she stops, turns and looks back for one last time at the house and the workmen. Her voice is breaking:

'That was our house, children. Never forget how they stole it away from us. They're all bastards, every single one of them.'

She turns, letting go of my hand, and quickly walks on.

✱

A few weeks after our conversation, I'm watching from the window at Post Office Cottage as the van pulls up outside. There's a SOLD board at our gate. A spiteful frost turns the grass to icy shards. Nic is helping Freddy and Grace into their seats in the back of the car.

The man locks the back of the removal truck. I watch from the front door, then I turn to lock up. The massive, inch-long iron key rattles in the latch. I reach out to grip and turn it. The hand is static and useless. I try in vain to force it round in the lock, but after a minute the key just falls out, clattering on the wet flagstone.

Pitter-patter footsteps. Grace has got out of the car and she's walking towards me, up the gravel path.

'Daddy, come on. Everyone's waiting for you.'

I'm breathing hard, exhaling clouds. I'm trying to pull myself together. Grace is looking up at me quizzically. Her jaw has dropped and her mouth is open. She sounds shocked.

'Daddy, are you *crying*?'

'No, darling. I'm just sweating a bit because I can't get the key to turn.'

'Oh. Would you like me to do it for you?'

I nod. Grace scrabbles on the flagstones by her feet for the key. It's absolutely enormous in her hand.

'Daddy, this key is really, really heavy.'

I lift her up as best as I can, gripping her tight under the arms with the crooks of my elbows. I have to be careful not to pinch her.

'Bit higher, Dad. Lift me up higher.'

I give her directions and she guides the key into the lock.

'I'm ready to turn it now, Dad.'

'Towards the drawing room window... OK, so as you do that, I want us both to make a wish. Repeat after me...'

Grace repeats after me, word for word, as she slowly locks the front door: 'Thank you, Post Office Cottage.'

OAKHAM, RUTLAND, 2004

The same hands, five years later, are now battered from use. The plastic gloves covering them have worn away from several of my fingers, exposing the metal skeletal framework.

I'm in our bedroom at the new house, a five-bed brick brute on an estate. Jean uses two of the bedrooms as a living room and bedroom. Every house down the street looks exactly the same. Identical cars are parked on identical driveways.

So, we've had to sell Hambleton. We're kind of devastated by that – that cottage embodied everything that is unique and distinctive about how Nic and I are together. It is us. But we are pragmatic about it – the situation is what it is and we have dwindling options.

Moving in with Nic's mum is never the preferred move but it is necessary. Angela herself understands this. She knows about these kind of choices. She knows we have no choice.

One hand has jammed again. I tap the battery box on the casing with the fingertips of my other hand to get it working.

There are no bandages on my face now. I have had more facial surgery. They've taken bone from my shoulder and created a structure for my nose to hang on. It's a slight improvement on the original 'flap' model, but my mouth is still very damaged. It's just a gaping hole, with no lips, top or bottom. My cheeks are badly scarred and grafted.

Once I get my hand working, I carefully unscrew the lid from a pill drum. This takes me five full minutes; it's not easy. I take the tablets to my en-suite bathroom. There I lift the lid of the toilet, tip all the drugs down it, then I hit the flush.

Car outside. Door slams. From the en-suite window, I see Nic walking to the front door. It opens. I hear Nic say: 'Hi, Freddy. Whatcha watching?'

'*Power Rangers Astro Delta Megazord.*'

'Again?'

'Where's Gracie?'

'Out with Nan.'

'Where did you go, Mum?'

'Pharmacy. I had to get Dad's tablets, but they'd run

out of one packet, so then I had to go to Boots, in town.'

Nic puts her bag down on the sofa next to Freddy then heads to the kitchen to make a pot of tea. As she is filling the kettle, she suddenly stops and goes back into the sitting room. Freddy has his hands in her bag and is about to open the packet of drugs from the pharmacy. Delving down deep in the bag, she pulls out the chocolate lolly that she knows he's looking for. She finds a parking penalty notice stuck to the lolly – our disabled pass had fallen on the floor of the car.

Here is a list of the tablets Nic has to order and re-order for me: hydrocortisone, penicillin, co-codamol, aspirin, ambien, valium, simvador, codeine, warfarin, simvastatin, amias, candesartan, otmomize. Some of these are just once a day, others more often. Each has to be ordered, collected, brought home and then distributed into a fat opaque plastic carrier that has the days of the week printed on it. Then there are plasters, bandages, arm fixes, hand fixes, leg repairs, cotton wool, stump socks, E45 cream, silk leg stump covers, new gloves for my hands, batteries for my arms, chargers for those batteries, earbuds, a thousand tissues, a million straws, a billion cold drinks... and so on.

Sometimes I try and save Nic the job of putting the drugs into the dispenser. I get all the packets out on the bedspread upstairs, and I try to pop the little pills out of their foil pouches with my myoelectric hands. If I'm careful and methodical I can just about manage this, but to do it properly, I have to go very slowly. It's a bit like cooking every grain of rice individually, or mowing the lawn and then going round to pick up each single blade of grass. More often than not, the tablets jump out of their little holes in the packets and go spinning on to the floor, disappearing under the bed, or behind the wardrobe.

I'm continually finding one or other of the drugs has been left out. Then either Nic or I must go back to Oakham to try and persuade the pharmacist to reissue something or other. There's a more or less constant to and fro to try and get it right.

The packets are put away in a cupboard that neither the children nor I can reach, so when there's one missing from my plastic dispenser, I have to call on Nic to find it. Every day, there's some issue – something's either run out, or fallen out, or not been included by the pharmacy, or gone down the sink or toilet.

This is all aside from the actual effect of all those tablets on my body. Their toxic combination makes my mood fluctuate between bright, over-energetic spells and a morbid despair. If I miss my hydrocortisone, or take it too late, I find myself dropping off to sleep in the middle of the day. Self-respect seeps out of me.

I hear Nic's footsteps on the stairs. Quickly, I put the empty pillbox on the bedside table. She appears in the doorway.

'Hiya!' I try to smile.

'How was your day?' she asks.

'Two novellas, three plays and a screenplay. Yours?'

'Good. It was...' She looks at the empty pillbox. 'Not again?'

For a moment, we both listen to the toilet cistern running in the background. Nic's tone is firmer when she says: 'Tom, you can't keep doing this.'

I can't look at her. 'Why do I need them anyway?' I say.

And then we go through it again. The sad litany of drugs, what damage and destruction they're mitigating. My spleen and adrenal glands gone. An antidepressant that makes me feel like a zombie: no highs, no lows, just a wave of beige sludge.

'What, am I so unbearable without these?'

'Yes. Yes, absolutely, you are.'

We glare at each other. After a long pause, Nic says: 'I'll get you some more tomorrow. Where's your exemption card?'

'Don't know.'

'Well, I'll have to find it then, won't I?'

I shrug, and she starts to walk out of the room.

'In the drawer with the fuses...' I call after her.

✱

Grace turns seven. Freddy is now four and a half. They are confident, noisy, active little kids – everything they

253

should be. They are in and out of the house all day, being taken to this place and that. Grace has her primary school routine and Freddy has just started nursery school.

I rely too much on Nic. It's suffocating her. She's trying to work out a way of getting back into employment, but the restrictions and pressures on her are immense. The children are always demanding her attention: they want her to play with them, to sit and watch a video, or bake them a cake, or walk into town, or make a den in the garden and hide. They want her to take them to play centres, cinemas, fast food restaurants, swimming baths, forests, bike shops, scooter parks, zoos, toy superstores, museums, beaches, dance lessons, karate lessons, parties, ice cream shops, model train stores, markets, friends' houses. They want to be dropped and picked up at all hours of the day and evening, for all kinds of obscure reasons and activities. All with zero budget. One day Grace is into S Club 7; the next she wants the latest album by Blue. Even Freddy is alternating daily between the Fimbles and Power Rangers. It's all very normal, and exhausting. The Tom Ray Trust money which had accumulated as a result of Nic's golf club speech, from the Rutland Water fun run and from occasional donations by strangers and well-wishers, allows us to carry on employing Suzanne, a brilliant nanny, from nine to five on weekdays, allowing Nic some temporary distance from all the flak. Most nights, she gets a handful of hours of broken sleep if she's lucky.

It's impossible to get a routine. Every day is different, with frequent visits to the limb centre in Leicester. My myoelectric arms seem to need constant attention, with broken battery housings and fragile, sensitive electronics. I am one of the very few people in the country who use them, so not many know how to fix them when they break. Every repair involves the hand or arm being sent off into the ether (possibly Germany) for periods of weeks at a time.

So when Nic tries to forge a new working partnership with her friend Sarah, there's tension. On the one hand, we could do with the money, but on the other, I'm conscious that I'm in danger of becoming even further isolated. I know that building a routine will be the only route out of the chaos in my mind. This starts with taking a shower on my own. I have an adapted en-suite bathroom, but it's still awkward and time-consuming. I sit in a chair on wheels and push levers on the wall to get soap and shampoo. There is an electric air drying system but it takes ages, so more often than not I just use a towel between my arm stumps to soak up the worst of the water, then put on my clothes while I'm still damp. When Nic helps me, the whole process takes twenty minutes, but on my own, it takes an hour and a half. If I drop anything while I'm in my wheelchair, I'm stranded.

Disabled. I'm starting to understand the true meaning

of that word. For me it means that when things stop, when I can't do something, I have to wait until Nic shows up.

I drink a bit, when I can. It's the one remaining luxury. Just wine, a glass or two of an evening – although for obvious reasons, Nic and her mum don't encourage this. I'm still taking serious amounts of tablets and the combination with even small amounts of alcohol cannot be advisable.

There is tension in the house. My mood fluctuates terribly. Nic has the kids to consider, plus her mum, who has her own issues and concerns. She ends up in the middle, trying to sweep up after all our petty arguments and tiffs. None of these are serious, and there are very few bust-ups between the three of us – but the long-term effect grinds us down.

It occurs to me that perhaps this is time to grow up. I'm forty-five years old. Like it or not, I can no longer rely on others to sustain me. I might be severely disabled, but it's just not going to be reasonable to rely on Nic to keep me. I'm just going to have to be stronger, more independent; more resilient. Otherwise, the next victim of what has happened to me will be Nic – or our marriage.

It's about what you can do, not what you can't. I can still walk, albeit on prosthetic legs. I have these amazing robotic arms. All I have to do is to learn more. It is not beyond me, I just need a plan.

✳

I'm silent, nervous. Nic is at the wheel of our people carrier. We're on the way to Leicester. The BBC has got hold of our story and has asked us for a radio interview. I'm the kind of person who usually loves to talk, but we're not really sure what to expect. Nic interrupts my train of thought:

'I hope you're going to be more communicative when we get there.'

I tell her I don't know what I'm going to say.

'It's easy, it's an interview – you just wait for them to ask you a question, you think about it for a second, then you answer. Job done. It's kind of exciting, really, when you think about it.'

She's right about that. We've both grown up listening to John Peel – his was the voice of late night radio for the entirety of our student years, and he is the epitome of everything that's good about modern music journalism. Lately, he's broadened out into mainstream broadcasting with his programme *Home Truths*, which has a reputation for high-quality coverage of amazing true life stories... like ours.

I remember plenty of late nights, especially when I was at Exeter University, when Peelie's dry, sardonic voice was my only companion. He'd play all the tracks that nobody else would, from The Undertones to Siouxsie and the Banshees (still Nic's style icon), to The Clash, to my great hero Tom Waits. It was sometimes hard to love everything he played, but he did it with such consistent casual grace that listening to his show just became an essential part of the daily routine.

We're shown into a studio at BBC Radio Leicester and wired up with headphones in a cramped booth. It's an old-fashioned set-up, with a PA and an engineer giving us the thumbs-up through the glass. Then that distinctive voice of John Peel's comes down the line, and we've started. He's immediately our best friend. He's been around and part of the national psyche for so long that he just seems like a mate. His down-to-earth approach makes it easy to identify with what he says.

'I understand there was a time when you suggested to Nicola that she should abandon you. Is that right?'

Nic and I exchange a look in the booth. I can hear the heavy intake of my breath in my headphones as I reply: 'She's obviously a very special person to me and anybody... in my position... where you see that person... having to... give up so much of themselves... to look after you, you think...'

I turn and look at Nic, then continue: 'You think, they deserve a lot better.'

Peel jumps in: 'But did you, Nicola, in those dark nights of the soul, did you ever think it might be a good idea?'

Nic sets her jaw and stares at me. She says firmly: 'The

thought of leaving never really occurred to me until Tom brought it up – so we sort of go round in this little ritual dance now and then…'

'It still comes up, does it?'

'Oh, he reminds me that I can leave at any point I want to, and I say, "why?" and that's it, really.'

Peel is good at conversation. It feels natural, positive, respectful – not mawkish. Although it's all done 'down the line' and we don't actually get to meet the great man face to face, his interaction is entirely intuitive, relaxed, intelligent and, as always, he has that beautifully natural way of expressing himself. It's as if we weren't sitting a hundred miles apart, but in the pub next to each other.

Nic and I don't say anything to each other in the lift down from the eighth-floor studio but I feel that we've communicated. And maybe we've succeeded in articulating the essence of our story to someone – a nation, or a small Radio 4 listening corner of it. Perhaps that will mean we don't feel so alone, in dealing with the aftermath.

✱

Despite moments of positivity, I find it near impossible to create any sort of enduring happiness in myself. My mood can plummet with seemingly no visible cause and I don't seem to be able to love anyone any more. I've become dangerously self-obsessed. There is so much anger in me,

I can hardly interact on a sociable level. I'm alone a lot. I'm frustrated at every turn, from the moment I wake up to the point when I go to bed. Everything I need, want or try to do goes wrong, gets broken, or ends up in a mess. Everything is fucked. It's very much like I've been in a war. I'm caught in an enduring loop of PTSD.

I still never look at myself in a mirror. It's easy, when you get used to it, but it has its drawbacks. Trying to work, and just to be a normal member of society, I have to make myself reasonably presentable. Nic dresses me every morning, but I have a tendency to look a bit dishevelled after a while, a bit scruffy. I'm constantly knocking things over, breaking and spilling stuff. So I can't keep clean, or even wash myself when it all gets too messy. I also drool continually. All of this impacts on my self-confidence, and on my self-image as Nic's husband. In many ways, I'm more like her child.

I realise I've stopped relating to her. I have become so wrapped up in my own physical and emotional situation, our relationship as a couple has become marginalised. Increasingly, I find it hard to be loving or tender. Nic has given me everything, she has sacrificed so much – the least I could do would be to demonstrate some affection. But I find myself emotionally and physically incapable. I can't even kiss her – I don't have lips any more. When I try to hug her, my ridiculous half-arms won't even wrap around her tiny body.

We lie in bed together, back-to-back. The lights are out but we're both awake. I turn over and put my half-arm across her shoulder. Nic is tired and sad. She lies still, as if she's asleep – but I know her eyes are open. She doesn't stir. I turn away from her then a few moments later, I feel her sobbing.

The next morning, after breakfast, she's putting out my pills in the plastic dispenser. I want to talk to her about the way we are (or aren't) together, but I don't even know how to start the conversation. I hover (stagger) in the doorway, then turn, leave and slowly climb the stairs.

Another day. I'm trying to get up on my own. I'm sitting on the edge of the bed, I've got my arms on and I'm trying to put on my leg-liners. I have a hard time sliding them down into my prosthetic legs. It takes several attempts and I get frustrated. I hear the front door close downstairs, so I stagger to the window. I see Nic's mum taking Grace and Freddy off to school. I watch them crossing our driveway.

'Look up...' I find myself saying, out loud. They don't.

Across the road, there's a piece of scrubland next to a small fenced-off electricity sub-station. There are some boys kicking a football against the fencing there. Freddy, without thinking, drops his book bag on the drive and runs towards them. Jean calls after him, but he takes no notice. The boys kick the ball to him and he passes it back. They all laugh. I smile. Then I see Jean

going over, grabbing his hand and yanking him back
onto the road. He's protesting, but she's wagging her
finger at him, giving him the third degree. She pulls him
back towards the car. All the time his feet are moving
one way, his head is turned in the other direction. But
his friends have gone.

I'm sitting at the dining table in the kitchen, alone. Nic
has gone out, trying to pick up more freelance production
work. Breakfast is usually toast and Marmite, which Nic
cuts into long, thin strips. Because all the skin is grafted
at my tiny hole of a mouth, it has no natural flexion, so I
can't eat big stuff, or get a spoon in. So when Jean puts
out a bowl of cornflakes for me instead, as she has this
morning, I'm stumped. The milk would drip all down
my front and the spoon's too big anyway so I just sit and
look at it. I sip my coffee through a straw, although by
now it's gone cold. I stare at my daily tablet box. 'The
Drugs Don't Work' by The Verve has always been one
of my favourite tunes. I used to listen to it at full blast, up
at Hambleton, now I think about it every time I have to
swallow more tablets.

Half an hour later, I'm in the dining room, in front of a
laptop computer screen. It's blank. I can hear the ticking of
my mother-in-law's clock on the mantelpiece. It's loud. I
don't know what to do, or how to occupy myself. When
Nic was at home, we could absorb ourselves in the daily
angst of trying to get by, set up medical appointments

and attend them, go shopping, ferry the kids around. Now that she's working, my options are limited. I don't want to be a couch potato, I don't want to watch TV. I've read everything, I've written too many scripts nobody will read. I don't feel like starting a new hobby, language or home business... I just feel like shutting down.

Despite myself, I tape a shopping list to my myoelectric arm and then shuffle through town to the Co-op. Somehow I arrange myself over a trolley, half-fill it with items that nobody wants, and push it all slowly along the aisle. At one point, I struggle with a piece of shrink-wrapped Cheddar, then end up destroying it in my vice-like hands. Bits of it go everywhere. I stop in front of the toothpaste, reaching up high to grab the good stuff. Suddenly all the packets are tumbling down over me, hundreds of them, all falling at my feet. A young shelf-stacker appears beside me.

'Sorry, chap. That wasn't what I intended.'

The young fella smiles. 'No problem, Mr Ray.'

I slide away, wondering how the lad knows my name. I've been in the local paper a lot. And Oakham is a small town. If you've lived here for a few years like we have, everybody knows you.

At the checkout, I'm very slow. The people in the queue around me just stare, watching me trying to put out each item. I can feel their eyes upon me; I think they're laughing at me. I bet they think I should be dead. At one point, a woman catches my eye. She smiles nervously then I look away.

I walk home, across the park, carrying my supermarket bags. I have to keep on stopping to adjust my grip. It's very tiring. I rest on a bench. The day is cold and grey. I look dejectedly around me. A young kid comes past with his mother. He stops in front of me, stretches out his arm and points directly at my face. I glare angrily back at him – I'm too emotionally exhausted to hide my feelings. The boy holds my gaze for a long time, trying to interpret the look I give him. After a few seconds, he looks away. The mother pulls the boy to her defensively. Picking up my shopping bags, I shuffle away.

I waste the rest of the day. I try to write, but end up just sitting in front of a blank computer screen. I wonder where Nic is. The clock ticks.

Later on, I'm upstairs in Freddy's room, going through his toy box. I play with a couple of Power Ranger figures, acting out a confrontation and inventing fighting talk for them. An hour after that, I go back to the blank screen downstairs and I start to type. It's a play – a radio comedy. I've got into the routine of writing scripts and sending them in unsolicited to the BBC Writers Room. That's how I remember my dad earning his living when he used to write for *Z Cars* and *Doctor Who*. Sometimes I get feedback, and once in a blue moon, a commission. I even wrote an Afternoon Play for Radio 4.

When I'm ready to print, I find we're out of paper. I check in the paper cupboard. Underneath the refill, I find the purple box. When I pull it out, I reveal Nic's box of paints and her artist's model – all the stuff I gave her years ago, still untouched in its packaging. I remember the carefree young woman who met me at Leicester railway station in 1995, and I compare her life then to what it has become.

In the kitchen, right at the back of a cupboard, I find a bottle of red wine. Cheap supermarket stuff. It's probably been there for a while. I find a corkscrew in the drawer and after seventeen attempts I manage to twist it into the top of the bottle. It's an awkward procedure, but you can tell by the careful technique that it isn't the first time I've tried it. I get the cork out and then I grip the bottle in my myoelectric hand, ready to rotate it so the wine tips slowly and elegantly into the glass I have ready. It isn't easy or perfect, but I manage it. I scrabble in the side of my manbag for an old straw that I can re-use. Gripping something as thin and bendy as a plastic straw is problematic, but eventually I get hold of it and drop it into the glass of wine. I have Nic's artist's model beside me on the table. I sit in my chair, with my glass of wine, staring at it. I clench the straw between my teeth and draw deeply on it. The wine in the glass disappears quickly; I empty it.

I pour a second full glass, wondering at my own dexterity. I don't know if it's the alcohol that's imbued me with physical confidence, but I'm good at this. After sucking the straw out of the glass, I spit it away. I pick the glass up in my plastic hand and attempt to drink it normally. Then I rest the nearside rim of it against the numb lower part of my mouth opening and tip it towards me.

It's a disaster. The red wine spills all down the lower part of my face where my chin used to be, all over the table and all down my clothes. I put the glass down into a sopping red ring on the table and wipe my face with my sleeve. I glare at the glass. I'm disgusted, angry, frustrated. I reach out and grip it with my hand... *whirr*... tight, then... *whirr*... tighter, then... *whirr*... very tight indeed. The grip is strong and I can't stop it. Suddenly the glass explodes upwards and outwards from my hand, showering my face and my throat. I'm covered in it. I start to laugh uncontrollably.

Nic arrives home an hour later. She's wearing her black suit; she looks office smart, as she always used to. I'm a bit scared of her. I can hear her calling my name from the door. There's the usual smile in the sound of her voice, but she's obviously very tired. When she opens the kitchen door, I'm sprawled across the kitchen table. My shirt is horribly stained with red wine and there's a pool of it still slowly dripping onto the floor. There's broken glass everywhere. I'm a bit drunk, a bit defiant. I've been rehearsing a speech, but now she's come in,

I've completely forgotten how it starts. For some reason I'd wanted to remind her about that first day, when we drove to Warwick...

Nic surveys the scene icily.

'You've cut yourself,' she says, very softly, without looking at me.

'Sorry.'

✱

The next morning, we're up early and this time Nic isn't going to her office. Today we're back at Addenbrooke's. I have an appointment with Mr Malata to find out what the next stage is in my facial reconstruction. I still have no nose to speak of, and I have a great wedge of split flesh for my lips. My mouth is permanently open and dribbling. There's a chin of sorts, although it's misshapen, and my ears look as if they've been nibbled by wild dogs.

All the way there, Nic doesn't speak to me. Mr Malata is his usual immaculately turned-out self, fastidious in his choice of words as he is in his selection of his silk tie and cufflinks.

'I have consulted with some of the world's most prominent maxillofacial plastic surgeons to see what can be done, Mr Ray, but I am afraid we are no further forward. Your situation is very unique and very difficult.'

'Are you saying there's nothing more that can be done?'

'It's exceptionally problematic. We could consider new revisions once your face has completely healed, but there is no doubt, Mr Ray, that this will cause further serious trauma both to your body and spirit, and we have to consider whether or not the results will justify the severity of that *distress*.'

He places a polite but heavy emphasis on that last word. No doubt he remembers the most recent operations – when he had to operate on my face with only local anaesthetic – as painfully as I do.

'Mr and Mrs Ray, I have to be completely honest about the reality of your situation. I am sorry, but the truth is that it's possible there is nothing more I can do for you.'

I haven't expected this. It comes as a shock. We've always been aware of Mr M's limitations when it comes to complex facial surgery. He's always been honest about what he can and cannot do, but up to now, there has always been the prospect of *refinements*. Now, even that possibility seems to be slipping away, and it's a bitter pill to swallow. Somehow, I've always imagined that Mr Malata could put my face back to something like normal. I've never expected perfection, but I've been hoping to end up with a face that might allow me to go back to some kind of office job.

'I could refer you to a specialist.'

I stare at him blankly, then reply: 'I'm sorry, I thought you were a specialist.'

'I am, Mr Ray. But...'

'But?'

'Not in facial reconstruction.'

This is hugely disappointing to me. I never realised that he wasn't a specialist in facial surgery. Why should he be? We started our journey together with him amputating great chunks of me. It simply never occurred to me to ask.

I make two more disappointing excursions into the dark world of plastic surgery. One involves a long drive to a meeting of a hundred leading consultants in Norwich, where I'm paraded in front of them all and examined, in case there's something Mr Malata has missed. Crowds of surgeons approach me, prod me, and pull my face. They all shake their heads and walk away.

A year or so later, after some tenacious detective work on the part of my mum, I am referred to the London Hospital to meet Iain Hutchinson. There's the same process of being politely and respectfully questioned and examined, poked and pushed around, but it comes to nothing. Hutchinson is one of the world's best facial specialists, but it seems my case is beyond even him.

There are many issues to consider. These are experienced consultants and one of the things they understand is just how gruelling and upsetting this kind of surgery can be. Just a single operation takes months out of a person's life. It has to be meticulously planned, organised, and followed up. This, just at the time when I am trying to get my life into some sort of routine, may be why they are not planning more work on my face. It's a nuanced decision. At the time, it's upsetting to be told that I'm going to have to look like this for the rest of my life. It deepens my anger and makes me feel abandoned. But with the benefit of hindsight, Malata and Hutchinson may have been right to leave me alone. They're probably taking a rounded view of my situation, seeing that I have a young family, and concluding I'm better off out of surgery, getting on with the rest of my life.

I lie in bed at night, trying to hold myself together. I've come a long way from the healthy, fit, energetic man I was at thirty-two, when Nic and I first got together. Now, I look like a train has run over me. I have no nose, a great big grafted chin that looks like it's been glued on to me, scarring everywhere. I've got rounded stumps where my hands and feet should be. Bits of me are hard, ugly and unfeeling, and not just on the outside. I don't know what Nic thinks about my face being like it is – she never says anything. I'm sorry I've become so ugly and repulsive. She is my one true love and she deserves someone better.

Things go from bad to worse. In 2004 we try to bring a case for medical negligence based on the long delay before the diagnosis of pneumococcal septicaemia. I hire an expensive firm of lawyers in Manchester to investigate and prepare a case. They engage a specialist consultant in clinical medicine to review all the notes. It's a costly business which was funded mainly by gifts from my family. There are few medical experts in Sepsis, so it takes time and money to get a written response from someone sufficiently qualified. The news is not wholly positive. Although the report highlights key mistakes and damaging delays, there's no specific evidence that, had these not occurred, my outcome would have been improved. There's no way of proving that I would not have ended up with the same amputations, had the diagnosis been quicker. The advice from the lawyers is, although we could bring a case, it might be contested – and we could lose. That would mean becoming liable for the health authority's legal costs, which would ruin us.

Nic and I are devastated. We got our hopes up: we thought a successful compensation claim might at least give us some financial security.

Nic is holding the letter. Her hand is shaking, although true to her nature, she's trying to find a way to be positive about it:

'They say one option would be to try and find another expert witness.'

'What, so they can drag it out even longer, and charge us for more work? Nic, there's no money left.'

It's true. We've exhausted all the cash from the sale of the house and the Trust money, trying to cover all the legal costs. Even after that, we've had to rely on donations from family.

'At least they understand our situation. They say they're only going to charge us half their normal fees.' Nic reads on. 'They're advising us to drop the case.' She folds the letter, looks up, and past me. She adds: 'I think I want to, too.'

The next day, I write a cheque for the legal fees and send it off to the solicitors, with a note to say we're done with the compensation claim.

Now we're down to zero. I decide to do something I've been putting off for a long time. I go to the computer, open up a blank page and then start to type:

Dear Dad…
Backspace.
Dear Father,
Thank you for the letter you sent some time ago. I've been very ill since December 1999, when I developed septicaemia and had to have my lower arms and lower legs amputated — I think my sister has given you some of the details. I'm enclosing a print of the diary my wife Nicola and I have been keeping to give you an idea of how things have progressed since then. Obviously, things have been very difficult, although after eight months in hospital, I'm home now and we're slowly trying to get started again.

Until the end of 1999, we had a successful video and conference production business together, and I developed a modest career as a voice-over artist and house husband, but since then we've been unable to work. Nicola and I have two young children, Grace and Freddy, so as you can imagine, life has been quite busy for Nicola, especially with daily trips to Addenbrooke's when I was in hospital. We're hoping to gradually get back to working again, but I still have a fairly full diary of physiotherapy appointments as I've only just started walking again recently. There will also be more operations over the next year or so as unfortunately my face is badly disfigured. So for the next few months we'll just be trying to establish some sort of routine – we moved recently, so we could reduce our mortgage and spend more time together at home. I've always been very interested to follow your career – Adam and I both trained as actors at Webber Douglas – especially at the National Theatre. I liked all that stuff you did at the Cottesloo. Myself, I always wanted to do radio plays. I used to love doing accents and dialects, but my mouth's all swollen up now and my lips are distorted, so the diction's mostly gone.

I don't believe in dysfunctional relationships any more. What I mean to say is, what's the sense and meaning of the brief years of our lives if we just fill them with silence? I was married before and then divorced – I do understand a bit about why relationships fall into such disrepair and why some things are just beyond fixing, even when you most need to. But time is so short and last year, in the time it takes evening to turn into night, without knowing a thing about it, I just sat down on the sofa and started to die. After all the money's been counted and after all the buildings have fallen down, bricks ground into dust, our relationships are eventually all we leave behind, all that is remembered. I don't think it does the soul much good to let things get so broken down and derelict.

Perhaps we could stay in touch and fill the silence.

Anyway, my situation has become more stable recently and Nic and I have taken steps to put our lives back together. But there's no denying this has been hard, and we're struggling now to keep our heads above water, financially…

Where do I imagine he will be, when he reads this? He did live in Hampstead, way back, in a mansion with an actress. Now I've heard they've retired to Norfolk. In my mind's eye, I see him pouring a glass of whisky, reclining in a leather armchair by a roaring fire, and reading on:

I hate to come to you with this, but I'm trying to put bread on the table, feed the family, and I don't know of a better way of dealing with a problem except head-on — so I'm asking you if there is any way you could…

Here, I start to falter:

Help us out — maybe let us have a loan — with interest of course — though not too much interest! Anyway, if you could, it would be really great. I hate myself for having to write this letter, but I really can't think of anywhere else to go...

I don't know how to end a letter like this so I just sign off simply:

From your son, Tom

I haven't seen my dad since 1971, but he lives on in my imagination. Now I picture him finishing the letter, polishing off his drink and rising from his armchair. He'll put his Waterford whisky tumbler down on a silver coaster, take a look around at his beautiful home then toss my note in the fire.

Looking back on this episode, years later, I will regret it deeply. This is undoubtedly the very lowest point of my downward trajectory. I have absolutely no respect for my father. Zero. I hate him with a passion and everything he stands for. In over forty years, he has never once expressed an interest in my welfare, apart from one letter to Intensive Care while I was in Peterborough Hospital. Why I thought he might ever respond, I really don't know. I certainly didn't tell my Mum I'd written that letter, she would have been utterly mortified by the very thought of it. I did share my secret with my sister, Nina, and she told me it was pointless, that there was no chance of my Dad replying. She remembered him better than I did, and she was convinced he was completely unfeeling, fundamentally unsentimental.

But I feel desperate. I don't know where to turn. I'm afraid of what the future holds for myself and my family.

★

Another meal. We're all eating silently in an atmosphere laden with tension. I'm the only one drinking wine. I slurp it noisily through my straw, deliberately trying to provoke a reaction. Grace is avoiding her vegetables.

'Eat your broccoli,' Jean tells her.

'Don't like it, won't eat it.'

'Well, it's good for you – it gives you iron. It'll help you grow big and strong.' Grace looks over the table at Freddy. Jean's attention follows hers: 'Don't hold your fork in your fist like that, Freddy. Look – hold it in your left hand.'

I wade in, without really thinking about it: 'It doesn't matter which way he holds his fork, he's a baby.'

This provokes a feisty reaction from Fred: 'I'm not a baby!' – which makes me laugh, and defuses the tension for a second.

Jean has a go at being positive: 'I'm just saying, we have to start as we mean to go on. What's he going to do when he goes to school? We don't want everyone to think he was raised by a pack of wolves, do we?'

I reach for more wine: 'It doesn't matter what anyone thinks.'

Nic lays her hand on my myoelectric arm and just says: 'Tom...' Then she stops, unable to complete her sentence.

Jean comes back with: 'Of course it matters – doesn't it, Freddy?'

'Well,' I say, 'it bloody well doesn't matter to me.'

We don't speak to each other like this; we never do. I don't know what's got into me. My mother-in-law doesn't back down. She's embarrassed by my outburst, but she sticks to her guns. She smiles thinly and says: 'Just because you don't care about manners doesn't mean they're not important.'

'In my world, they're not. I no longer have time for that sort of thing.'

'Fair enough, you can think what you like. But maybe manners are important to Nicola.'

By now, Nic has her head in her hands. But I rise to the bait. I get up and walk towards Jean: 'Oh, that's right. Go on, use your daughter against me, I know you like to come between us whenever you can. You do love a bit of control, don't you?'

Jean's not intimidated. 'I don't know what you mean by that. That's simply not true.'

At this, Grace shouts: 'Daddy!'

Jean's smile has disappeared. She looks briefly at Grace, then back at me. She doesn't speak. Nic starts to sob, silently. She gets up and leaves.

When I go upstairs, I find Nic sitting on the floor of the bathroom. She's rocking to and fro, her knees tucked in tightly. She never breaks down like this, she never cries. She's taken off the necklace that has my wedding ring strung on it – the one she's worn since the day I fell ill. She's fiddling with the chain.

'Sorry,' I say.

After a long silence, she looks up. 'I can't go on like this, Tom.'

'It's not me – it's *her*,' I say.

But Nic just shakes her head. 'She's just trying to protect me. Me, Grace and Freddy. That's what she does, and now she's done everything she can. We all do everything we can. We walk on eggshells around you, Tom. You only see how this thing affects you – you don't, *won't*, see how it's hurting everybody else.'

I'm thinking very quickly now. My heart is beating fast. Everything – my whole life – is at stake right here, right now.

'It *is* her. She's stealing you and the kids from me, Nic. No, it's worse than that – she's turned me into one of the kids. It's as if you and your mum were the adults and I'm just another baby to be spoon-fed and cleaned up after. It feels like the last bit of my being a man is disappearing. My last bit of dignity. That's it then. I've lost everything – I can't work, can't earn money, can't give you or Grace and Freddy the things I want to, the things I never had... I can't even kiss them goodnight or hold their hand – or even smell them, Nic. I can't even smell you... or make love to you.'

Nic stares at me and bites her lip. There's a long silence, then she says: 'I can't, Tom. I can't do that anymore.'

I shake my head; I look at the floor. But Nic's still staring at me, and she goes on: 'Look at me, Tom. I'm empty, wrung out... I just want us to get through the days and to get into some kind of secure place – to find some sort of reality that isn't this. Where if we can't ever be truly happy, at least we can have some happiness around us.' She takes a breath, wipes her eyes with her sleeve before adding: 'You, Grace and Freddy are everything to me. And I'll never stop loving you, Tom, never stop believing in you – but I can't make love to you. I can't be that woman any more. I've seen and done things that no lover should ever have to see or do. I don't dream like I did before, Tom. I don't dream at all. I just... do. And try to get through the days.'

Nic looks away from me. She is silent for a long time, then she says: 'With your black moods, and the way you

279

hate everybody and everything... God knows, you have a right to – but we aren't your enemy. Not me, Freddy, Grace, not even my mum – we're the ones who love you. We're the ones who go through that pain with you. We share it. Every second, every minute, every hour, every day. But all we get back from you is more pain, more anger, more hurt. It's getting so I can't – *we* can't – breathe any more when you're around – you just seem to suck the air out of every room you walk into.'

This is starting to sound like my mum talking to my dad. I'm stunned. Scared. All I can do is to stare at Nic. I'm shaking.

'Don't leave me, Nic. Please don't leave me.'

'Don't you get it? We're not leaving you, Tom. That's not going to happen. It's the other way round: you're leaving us.'

Nightlight: Freddy's bedroom, hours later. Freddy is asleep amidst a rumple of covers. Nic is sitting, fully clothed, on the edge of the bed. By the pale light her cheeks are glistening with silent tears. I resolve in that moment to get help.

✱

Autumn comes on. It's chilly and damp, but the colours around us are pure and beautiful. The leaves of the trees around Rutland Water are golden, red and brown. The lake itself is a steely grey and the sky is a deep, reassuring blue. The air is clear and fresh. It makes me feel good, filling me with a restless energy. We're embraced by a natural world that reaches out to us with this strong healing quality. But I'm broken. There is a hole inside me. At dawn, I ease our people carrier slowly down the hill, creeping up to the water's edge. I turn the engine off, and stare. There is no one else around. The sun is slowly rising above the horizon on the eastern hill of the reservoir. I open the driver's door of the car and swing my legs out. I walk slowly towards the wooden bench, continuing straight past it to the very edge of the water. I take four long steps into the lake. I stop, look down at the water lapping around my false legs, then I move forward again, deeper into the mud, feeling the freezing sensation rise to my knees. I stand and breathe heavily. I clench my jaw. I'm starting to shiver.

The water's now up to my waist and for the first time, I start to think in a rational way about what I'm doing. But it's hard to think straight. Everything's twisted in my heart and in my head, and nothing comes. *Nothing.*

Down by the water. *In the water...* I'm a few feet in, and I'm looking into the murky darkness, smiling. My shoes have disappeared into the silt and the mud, but there's a single shaft of sunlight and something shining down there.

A starfish.

OAKHAM, RUTLAND, 2006

'Walking on the Moon'

Freddy's playing football with some mates, down on the bit of scrubland surrounding our estate. It's flat and featureless, the grass is scorched, patchy; the earth is bald in places. The road running past is busy, so the most important thing is not to kick the ball anywhere near the cars. Or, of course, the electricity sub-station with all the deadly equipment inside it. Touch that, and you're dead. Freddy kicks the ball to one of his mates, but the boy has already noticed me approaching. He swings his foot at the rolling ball but with his eyes on me, and he slices the football straight over the sub-station wall.

Freddy's mates start laughing, then begin walking away, shaking their heads. Freddy stares at the sub-station wall in disbelief. 'My ball,' he mumbles.

I glance at the wall, with its razor-wire top, then look back at Freddy. I turn and walk away.

Freddy is crestfallen. Weeks and weeks, he had to save up for that ball. Now he's lost it, for good. *Any other dad*, I'm thinking. *Any other dad...*

Freddy does a double take: he absolutely can't believe what he's seeing. I'm shuffling back down towards him, hobbling with two steel stepladders and trailing a blanket. Behind me, Freddy can see Grace following – she too is completely intrigued.

I reach the sub-station wall, lean one set of steps flat up against it, then the other face-on so I can climb them. I take a deep breath and place my artificial foot on the first rung. Then I take each rung at a time. Uncertain, scared, wobbly... I don't know if I can do this, or if it's going to work – but I'm determined to try.

'Dad?' Freddy sounds scared, incredulous.

'It's all right, son. I'm just going to get your ball back – that's all.'

I hear Grace shouting for her mum. Up, up, up I go. It's difficult. Rotate hand, lock it, grip, take a step... Repeat. Don't forget to let the grip go before you move upwards or you'll... Move your other hand. Rotate and lock it. Lift leg. Step. Careful! My concentration and focus is tiger-fierce. This is a test. I cannot, *will not* fail.

At the top I turn, reach downwards. Grabbing the top of the other set of steps with my myoelectric hands, I heave them up and swing the weight of them over the top of the wall.

Bang, clatter, scrape, crash!

It's all right – the eagle has landed, and upright, just as I planned it. I slowly drag the blanket I'm carrying over my shoulder, letting it drop onto and cover the razor wire. Freddy is staring up at me, open-mouthed.

By now, Nic and Grace have run out from the house and are on the other side of the wall, next to Fred. Nic sounds terrified: 'Tom, what are you doing? Get down from there, you maniac!'

From the top of the ladder, I frown at her. I swing one artificial leg onto the steps inside the sub-station, test my weight on the top rung then shift my entire body over the top. There is an audible intake of breath from my family. I step slowly backwards, downwards, into the sub-station. It's all going well, but halfway down I miss a step, lose my balance, and go crashing down onto the gravel.

'Tom?' Nic is calling out to me.

There's a silence.

'Tom!'

'I'm all right!'

The football's in the corner – the electrical bit is just a disappointing metal box in the corner. I walk over, pick up the ball and boot it back over the wall. From the outside I hear screams and applause.

Nic, Freddy and Grace hear the clatter as I right the

287

ladder again and start slowly climbing out of the sub-
station. Freddy's already holding the ball – I can see him
beaming up at me as I reach the top of the steps: 'That
was awesome, Dad!'

Nic is nodding in agreement. I rise on my artificial legs
at the top of the ladder and shout at the top of my voice:
'*Never surrender!*'

2006-2017

Snapshot 1

It's November 2006, on a rainy Monday morning. I'm sitting in the student cafe at De Montfort University, Leicester. It's busy all by me. Nic is two years into a part-time Fine Art degree and I'm waiting in front of a large latte until she's finished her classes.

I'm trying hard to fit in. Being out like this on my own is sometimes a risk, physically speaking. Think Lee Evans on a skateboard, in fog – severe disability turns you into one of life's ice-skaters.

I have a big white plastic carrier bag by my false legs with one re-wired prosthetic arm in it, plus a pair of myoelectric hands. False hands. I've just picked them up from the Disablement Services Centre at the local hospital. My prosthetic hands are always breaking, so I often have to drive these faulty bits of me into Leicester for running repairs. *Help*. It's become a lifestyle.

The hands have skin-tone silicone gloves on them to give a natural appearance, but their inner workings are skeletal steel. I'm *Skellig*-like. I have to re-charge them every night by my bedside. Red light green light in the darkness. When they are working, they grip and rotate, but they are often broken so I'm more or less constantly making this trip to arrange and collect repairs. The arms themselves are no less reliable, there are frequent issues with fitting and fixing faults. Hmmn.

But that's done for today and my repaired limbs are resting against the chair leg, in the cafe. I'm surrounded by young university students, and at the age of forty-five feeling a bit out of place. To be honest, I often feel like this. And yet, I like the way no-one seems to take much notice of my disability here. It's a given. Amongst these younger students, in the city, I feel invisible, and that suits me just fine.

As part of her coursework, Nic has made a video installation of the sun and the moon and she's setting it up in the gallery across the road. I love the fact that she is finally getting to be the artist she always wanted to be. I don't want her to be fixing plasters on me, I want her to be painting her dreams. Good dreams, for once.

I am in a constellation of strangers and now I'm basically

powered by electricity. I close my eyes, reminding myself that we are all essentially just stardust. The traffic outside, the breeze in the trees and the clouds in the sky slide by. The day breathes slowly in and out, grey white light dividing itself into a billion fragments of sound and vision. There is feeling and non-feeling. A million tiny splinters of sadness and ice pass through my soul and my brain every second. They delight and scare me. I try to ignore them.

I'm often waiting these days, and my world is occasionally excessively weird. There are two pairs of prosthetic legs in my car boot and I'm drinking my coffee through a straw.

But I'm trying to repair myself.

It can be extremely hard for me, and I often feel desperate. Jagged. Lost.

I'm OK. I have to be OK.

Snapshot 2

My writing takes me places. I can type on a laptop with the right finger of one prosthetic hand; it's slow but I can manage it. I have the gift of time, lots of ideas and a strong desire to make sense of this fractured world that I now inhabit.

I'm not disabled when I'm writing.

I'm free.

In 2004 I write *Daybreak*, a play for radio, and BBC

Radio 4 commission it for broadcast. It's a curious fantasy dream-piece based on a day when the sun fails to rise. I'd conceived the central idea as an allegory for a marriage that fails, so there are just two characters caught in an extended private tragedy but also living it against the live backdrop of a single day's unfolding global catastrophe. The whole idea is really neat, and by the time the BBC Writers Room have made me redraft the script one hundred and twenty times, I'm impressed by the finished product. The broadcast has a chilling intimacy to it, a rare and special feel in the way the couple interact. I'm very proud of it, and I make a point of being at the recording so I can learn as much as possible about the radio drama process. It couldn't be better.

Other opportunities follow. In 2005 I write a sweet short little comedy drama for the experimental channel BBC7. It's called *Moonlight Serenade* because at its heart it features the famous Glenn Miller tune, and it's a weird kind of WW2 ghost story about a Lancaster bomber that takes off for a mission over Germany but returns without its crew. It's a beautiful, haunting piece, with marvellous stiff-upper-lip characters, lots of RAF bravado, and great poignancy. I want to make people smile, laugh, wonder and reflect on the incredible bravery and resilience of ordinary men.

We record it in London and this time I insist on acting one of the parts. I really enjoy this. It's hilarious.

I make writing connections. Sitting at home, poor disabled me, I just keep on turning out scripts. Unsolicited, I send in dummy episodes to *The Archers,* I get invited into the BBC in London to try out as a writer for CBBC's *Kerching!* and for the prime-time soap *EastEnders.* I'm really attracted by the idea of being able to earn a regular income from writing, so I throw everything I can into these try-outs. They represent a massive chance for me to completely re-set my lifestyle.

But it's hard work. Often, I'm required to travel, then stay overnight in unfamiliar places. As a quadruple amputee, I'm never really sure that I can physically do what I have to. There's always that underlying fear. The simple idea of me managing by myself in a hotel environment is incredibly challenging. Nic has to stay home with the kids, so I'm out on my own – as it were, on a creative tightrope.

I force myself to be bold about it. I have to be.

I have a policy nowadays, a way forward: when someone offers you something new, don't hesitate - *just say yes*. Just go with it, and see where it takes you.

I go back to BBC Birmingham where I'm invited for a whole week to work as a writer with the team that produces the TV drama *Doctors* for BBC1. This is basically an extended masterclass in how to storyboard and write, with access to experienced senior producers and a chance to devise an episode all of my own. The opportunity is priceless, although once again, the logistics of being away from home and independent are very challenging.

By 2008 I'm on a roll. Eight years into my strange disabled life, I'm invited to be Writer in Residence at a Radio Drama workshop at the Arvon Foundation in Shropshire. I spend a glorious intense week there and produce a radio play called *House Arrest,* another piece based on a relationship break-up. I try to make my writing real, relevant, hard, uncompromising. My play is chosen to be produced and broadcast on BBC Radio3, and I do an interview with journalist and poet Ian MacMillan to accompany it.

It all sounds great. I'm trying really hard to do all this, but it's very, very difficult to operate independently. I fall over a lot. For example, for the Arvon Centre week, I have to stay in rural Shropshire. I have to drive deep into the country, I have to look after myself for a week there, as well as meeting all the exacting daily writing challenges. I'm basically climbing Everest, physically, creatively, spiritually. My heart sweats.

I want to change my life so much. As disabled and disfigured as I am, I really want to fulfil my potential. But I over-reach myself, and nearly have a breakdown on what turns out to be a nightmare of a journey home. I'm driving a hundred and fifty miles by myself and I get horribly lost.

Oh.

Snapshot 3

Reading this back now, it's clear that I have a habit of regularly re-inventing myself. This may well spring from a powerfully insecure childhood – my mum and dad fought like cats and dogs and that affected me badly.

I start to leave off the writing now, because although I am earning dribs and drabs, it is tough to get commissions. For example, I spend all my spare time in 2009 penning a crime novel titled *Apostle*, send it to one hundred agents, only to find that none of them will read it. *They won't even read it.* So, rationally speaking, as a parent and husband with bills to pay, there seems little point in devoting whole chunks of time to an activity that has zero return.

By now I'm working part-time in the local call-centre. In fact, thinking about it, I've already been doing this for four or five years. It's kind of heart-breaking, but entirely necessary. I could go on at length, but it's basically a factory process. I earn minimum wage, but the work means we qualify for Tax Credits, so it means we can just get by. I take orders for clothing, seemingly the same call over and over. There's a monthly catalogue, featuring trousers, T-shirts, blouses and skirts, shoes, swimwear, mostly aimed at the over 50s. The day I first walk in there, I really don't know whether or not I'll be able to manage, but as it turns out, it's simple. Sit. Put headphones on, log-in to a computer, wait for the calls, use the mouse. A hundred times a day, over and over.

So it's do-able. But only just, and it's not long before I'm looking around for something better.

A long time before, in my late twenties, I qualified as a teacher and when a job comes up at our local secondary school, I decide to give it a try.

Here I'm a Literacy Teacher, so I work with small groups of pupils to help them develop confidence in reading and writing. Many of the kids have issues with dyslexia, so it requires serious patience and a careful, individualised approach.

What a challenge. Walking in every morning to a huge new secondary school campus, setting up my classroom and making sure I have all my teaching materials ready, I have to be super organised and have all my wits about me. The kids all have their own problems and managing their behaviour as a disabled teacher can be difficult.

I make mistakes sometimes, but I learn fast.

The work has its good points and bad points. On the one hand, it has great purpose and there is nothing more useful I can think of doing with my time. Encouraging young people to overcome the barriers they have to reading and writing is such a great thing to do. Plus, I get a kick out of standing up in front of an audience and presenting information – I suppose in that sense, I am a bit of a show-off, so the constant requirement to lead classes and create my own mini-spectacle is a great new opportunity for me. Also, I really enjoy the actual business of teaching, the intense kind of interaction, and the imperative to constantly improvise on my feet. That need to always say the right thing. I get that, and I love doing it. The only real downside is that some of the pupils are disruptive and seek to undermine me, but that's all part of the territory and with time I learn the necessary skills to manage this and create energy in the classroom and a positive environment.

I like reading stories and poems to the kids. I love getting them to read to me. I make them do old-fashioned spelling tests, we practice writing letters and texts; we soak it all up, I encourage them to learn from their mistakes. My constant advice to them is, *less is more* – just write small amounts, but do it well, take it slowly, check your work, then check it again.

But then, just as I'm getting into my stride, they school year ends and it seems there's no funding to sustain my position going forward. In actual fact, there's no real explanation of this – it's just what I glean, on the grapevine. No-one has the courtesy to sit down and explain it, least of all the Head Teacher. This is so disappointing, as I have the idea that if I work at it I could develop towards being a full-time English teacher. Also, with the way I look, and my severe disability, it has taken a lot of courage to establish myself as a literacy teacher in what is indisputably a challenging environment – so to have it just disappear without explanation is more than galling.

After all that superhuman effort, I feel really disheartened.

By now, it's 2014. Back to the call centre then.

Snapshot 4

Later that year, my brother Adam dies. He has been living in Sydney, Australia, and develops stomach cancer. He does everything he can to try and fix it, including trips to Germany for experimental therapies – but he can't overcome it.

I stay up until the early hours watching a live link to his funeral ceremony. It's a difficult moment.

I am heartbroken.

Adam was funny, generous, hard-working, caring, sensitive, ambitious, inventive, skilled, artistic, friendly, determined. He was a terrific Dad, and most of all he was great company.

I loved him so much and although he's with me in my head always, now he's gone it feels like there is a big, big hole in the actual physical world where he should be.

Snapshot 5

I'm on a film set in Cottesmore, Rutland. For a few years now, we've been collaborating with our old friend Bill Clark on a movie about my Sepsis and its aftermath.

The film is called *Starfish*.

It's taken an age to finalise the script, to get the right

cast and crew, and to establish funding, but now that's all done and the cameras are rolling.

It's December 2015, and it's very, very cold. They've built the set inside a hangar at the RAF base, complete with a mocked-up hospital operating theatre, corridors, waiting rooms, etc. Nic is working as an assistant to the art director, so she's painting bits of the set and helping with props. I'm standing in as a body double for the actor Tom Riley, who is playing me in the movie.

It's a strange, powerful experience. We've spent so long trying to move on from sepsis and the catastrophe it brought into our lives, now suddenly we are re-living it.

All the nightmares, all the shock, all the pain.

I had thought about this before and wondered if it was right to do. On the one hand, we do of course want to leave it all behind and move on. I think most people would understand that. But on the other hand, we have a unique story to tell about sepsis, loss and love. Plus, the fact that Nic and I both come from creative backgrounds means that we are strongly motivated to be involved in the movie-making process.

It's a three week shoot and we're involved more or less every day. Nic painstakingly helps to recreate the operating theatre set, which is kind of my worst nightmare, as I went through some traumatic times under the surgeons' knives. But it's so interesting. Joanna Froggatt plays Nic in the movie and at one point she carries me up a flight of stairs – something Nic used to do every night when I came home from hospital.

Recreating that scene with Jo is very weird indeed. It makes me think hard and in a new way about everything that Nic did for me in those rehab years.

She absolutely saved my life, and mended me when I was broken. I will never forget that, nor the love and devotion she has shown me ever since.

The film lays our life bare. All the love Nic and I have for each other, but also the destructive impact of sepsis, the profound isolation of severe disability, the enduring grief, the effect on my mental health.

By now, I'm pretty damn tough, but there is a scene showing me walking into Rutland Water which never fails to make me cry. It makes me think about the man I was before sepsis.

That man is now gone.

But ultimately, the film tells a positive story about the capacity we have as humans to endure and recreate ourselves. When there is love in our lives, anything is possible.

Snapshot 6

Lancaster, January 2016. I've been worried about what my mum will think of the movie, but a few days after filming stops, we get an SOS message from my sister saying that mum is seriously ill. She's missed Christmas completely, she's taken to her bed and is refusing to see a doctor.

Cancer kills quickly, and it turns out that mum has been concealing the signs and symptoms for many months.

She is transferred to the local intensive care unit but she dies in hospital within two days.

I scolded her for refusing medical help, but the truth is she knew she was beyond saving. I should have understood that and let her be peaceful.

I held on to her arm in the last hour.

She was breathing very fast at the end.

Sometimes Mum's love was overpowering, but when I think about it now, it feels like she was trying to make up for the absence of my father by being somehow doubly present. There were times when he was too assertive, too angry, but – the song is sung now and we let mum go, with profound thanks for everything she did in her life.

A few days later, I am proud to speak at her funeral service but on top of losing Adam, I feel a huge void opening inside. Is this what being a grown up feels like?

Snapshot 7

Scoot forward. 2016. I'm watching TV at home. A re-run of *Grand Designs*, which I kind of love as a programme, but also kind of hate. On the one hand Kevin McCloud is almost exactly the type of man I always wanted to be

— articulate, stylish, savvy — but on the other, the house-building couples he follows are almost without exception infuriating. The fact that they appear to have money to burn never ceases to amaze and disgust; their material wealth and complacency seem staggering. Then again, the houses they create are generally wonderful, unique.

So anyway, here I am, fixating on another episode that I've probably watched and forgotten three times over already. Then the phone rings.

I always have to jump for the phone. It takes me time to pick it up from its cradle, then ten more seconds to select and press the answer button with my myoelectric hands. So often, by the time I've done this, the thing has stopped ringing and the person at the other end of the line has hung up.

This time, I just about get there, and it's my sixteen year old son Freddy:

'Dad, I'm lost.'

A beat.

'What do you mean, you're lost?'

'I mean, I'm lost, as in I don't know where I am.'

OK, I think. *Stay calm*, I tell myself. Gather information.

It turns out that Freddy has met a girl at a gig, travelled independently to visit her at home, then missed the last bus back. Apparently, he'd been standing at the stop with his hand raised, but the bus had driven straight past.

It's the kind of thing that has happened to all of us, but

in this part of the country, the distances can be huge and a person can soon find themselves stranded.

'So what can you tell me about where you are?'

'I'm at a bus stop. In the country.'

'This country?' At this point, I am trying to make it into a joke.

'Lincolnshire.'

Oh, that word. *Lincolnshire*. It falls into the conversation like an incendiary device. Lincolnshire's as big as Texas, it's wild and dangerous. I am instantly on my guard.

'Where in Lincolnshire? What's the town called?'

'I'm not in a town. I'm on a country lane, near a village. I don't know what it's called. Dad, it's getting dark.'

Oh.

So, we go round in circles like this for a minute or two, during which Freddy has time to tell me that his phone is running out of charge, then I have an idea. I get him to type the question 'Where am I?' into his iPhone, then it gives him his location.

Bang. Thank goodness for modern technology.

I get into my car, put my driving glove on, then head off into the evening darkness. By now, rain has started to fall.

An hour later, I'm getting pretty desperate, but I find him. He's sitting under the bus stop, perched on the kerb, shivering and wet.

He opens the passenger door and falls into the car.

I'm not the sort of Dad that would give his son a row in

this kind of situation, although maybe I should. I'm just so glad and grateful to have found him.

More than that, it occurs to me that this is kind of wonderful. It feels like a signal.

Because, there was a time when I was expected to die, to disappear and to be gone forever and not only did I not do any of those things, I've stuck around and rehabilitated myself to such an extent that I can rescue my son in an emergency. This is a massive step forward for me. I never had a Dad that would do that for me, and even as damaged as I am, I can still rally round and be really very useful for my son. It fills me with strength, pride and hope for the future.

I can be someone. It's all been worthwhile, after all.

'You wanna put a tune on, then?' I ask Freddy.

He swipes on his phone, and we play *OK Computer* by Radiohead very loud all the way home.

Snapshot 8

It's February 2017 and I am sitting in my car outside a unit on a trading estate in Melton Mowbray. I've driven ten miles or so from our home in Oakham, Rutland, it's a Saturday, and I'm trying to buy a wheelchair.

Not for me, you understand. I'm quite happy moving about on my false legs – oh, they hurt a bit and they don't fit very well, but I just about get by. No, this time the emergency is nothing to do with me.

The wheelchair is for Jean, my mother-in-law. She's been poorly since before Christmas and at eighty-two, she finds walking out increasingly difficult. Last December, she had a bad fall coming out of a screening of our film *Starfish*. She cracked her head on the concrete step of the Arts Centre cinema in Stamford and spent one night in hospital. Since then, at home with us, she has gone into sharp decline, and now, in an effort to get her at least semi-mobile again, I'm looking for a second-hand wheelchair.

Rural Leicestershire on a wintry Saturday; a pitiless grey-blind sky. It's quiet. Dead quiet. In fact, when I finally locate the Mobility Outlet on the trading estate, looking across from the empty car park, I can see that it's closed. I'm not surprised; I was half-expecting that. Any quest like this in our backwoods part of the country usually takes a degree of ingenuity. Shops are often closed, and even when they're open you often find they don't stock what you're looking for. You learn not to set out with great expectations. It's like managing disability. Stuff happens – you simply have to work your way through setbacks. Your challenge is to think around the problem and create your own solution.

There is the dry crunch of loose gravel under my tyres as I pull away. I point my car back towards the centre of town and consider my options. I'm already tired, I can't walk far, I have no idea where to find what I'm looking for, but I need to buy that wheelchair. Failure is not an option.

I park in the town centre, then instinctively head for the first charity shop on the high street. Not because I'm expecting to find what I'm looking for there, but because over the years I've learned that the people who run these shops tend to have both time to talk and excellent local knowledge. Age UK is cluttered and crowded. In every corner, standing against every wall, are the discarded possessions of those who no longer care, or who can no longer *take care*. Objects once loved now lie abandoned and purposeless, gathering dust. Pots, paintings, paraphernalia of all kinds seem to shy away from my gaze as my eyes dart around the room.

A diminutive lady in her seventies appears in front of me.

'I need a wheelchair...' I tell her, and she immediately asks if I'd like to sit down.

'And would you like a drink? Tea, perhaps?'
I shake my head, smiling. *The very idea of tea. Although, come to think of it, maybe that would be nice...*

'No – the thing is...' and off I go, explaining about my mother-in-law, telling the story, trying to get her onside.

Turns out, they don't have a wheelchair. Apparently they sell within hours, and my timing is not good.

'But you could try Charlie down at Ancient & Modern – he sometimes picks up things like that. Or, he'll be able

to look out for a wheelchair and ring you as soon as.'
She gives me directions, and I walk for ten minutes to find the shop.

Once again, inside it's crammed full, and this time it's mostly old furniture. Charlie has two wheelchairs. I choose the lighter one – it has smaller wheels but looks a lot easier to manoeuvre. The deal is done quickly but Charlie will only take cash, so I have to fetch that and drive my car round from the town centre where I parked it.

Cash machines are difficult. I can manage the buttons with my prosthetic hands, but I can't retrieve my bank card from the slot once the transaction is complete. Sometimes, I can't pick up the cash, either. So, on this occasion, what I do is turn to the guy behind me in the queue, explain my predicament and ask for help. I get mixed reactions when I do this, so I'm never quite sure of the outcome, but this time it works well.

I stagger back round to the shop, hand over the cash, and Charlie packs the wheelchair into the back of my Ford Focus. Job done. Later on that day, Nic takes her mum out to the shops and the wheelchair turns out to be really useful. That's a typical day in my odd little life. We bump along.

Snapshot 9
I'm in Manchester, it's a Sunday in summer 2017, and the music is exquisite.

STARFISH

The Whitworth Gallery, in an upstairs gallery space – huge, airy, resonant. Expansive wooden floor, the biggest picture windows I have ever seen. Endless views of the park outside, the tops of trees moving like a green ocean, reaching into the distance, waves of seething leaves.

A crowd has gathered, I sense a performance is about to begin. I have time on my hands, so I choose a seat. I just drop down into one, like it's all been planned (which it hasn't). I'm casual about it.

Beethoven in my feet. A String Trio. 'Opus 9 no.1 in G Major'. Ah, that sound, rooted, then soaring, coming up through my shoes. That beautiful sense of organisation and perfect symmetry, that liquid momentum in the air, so perfect. Suddenly, for several consecutive moments, with this music and with the views through the windows, I feel complete.

It's so perfect, I could almost cry.

And I am happy anyway today, because Nic and I are here to bring Grace back after her first year at university. She is studying Physics and Philosophy and we are so proud of her, but we are overjoyed at the thought of having her back with us at home, for a couple of months at least. It's like the planets are all coming back into alignment.

We help her clear out her hall room and Nic and Grace transfer the last year of university life into the back of our Ford Focus. Cardboard boxes full of books, clothes on hangers, files, posters. It's all packed in very tightly.

How amazing to have these grown up children, after everything we went through. How incredible it is that we have all somehow survived, somehow intact and somehow still together. I remember all that time I was in hospital after my Sepsis, when Grace was just two years old and my face was so bad she couldn't come to see me. Then, I was frightened we would never get back on terms with each other, and that I would lose my precious daughter. But I needn't have worried. Turns out, Grace has strength, intelligence, intuition, and is a profoundly caring person.

That's a lesson for us all. We stress far too much about things that could go wrong, or things we might lose – when in actual fact, outcomes are generally much more positive. *It is what it is and it will be what it will be. Don't worry about it.* That's what I tell myself, now.

Grace is bright, amused, obviously intelligent, but also pragmatic and intensely self-aware. She's downstairs, walking through the art gallery, hand in hand with Nic. Despite everything that was going on around her, throughout a turbulent childhood, she turned out to be brilliantly balanced, hugely capable, friendly and warm-hearted. She obviously has huge practical awareness and a fascination for the way that things work.

She just seems to get by, without ever having to fuss. If Grace was flying the plane and you were her passenger, you'd feel safe and happy.

I think back to those precious two years before my Sepsis, just after she was born, when I was at home full-time looking after her. I think I sensed it at the time, that I was so profoundly lucky. The bond you forge as a parent in those first years is so important, so vital – what Grace and I developed during that time was so strong that nothing could break it. Not even a profound personal catastrophe.

So we're good together now, even as she reaches twenty. We're friends, and it feels like Grace has a huge, exciting future to look forward to.

During university vacations, she works in our local Caffe Nero coffee shop. I like going in there when she's on shift. Grace is purposeful, organised, hard working. She's on the team. She brings me coffee.

Then Nic comes into the cafe with Freddy.

Sepsis broke me and I had to fight so hard to get back home.

But now I have my family around me. I've made it.

EPILOGUE

I feel older now. Both Nic and I have turned fifty-five, Grace is twenty, and Freddy is seventeen.

My brother and my mother are gone but they live inside me now, in my heart and soul. Their voices guide, soothe and console me. It's incredible how time passes. Bob Dylan was right, it truly is a jetplane; so much has changed in the last few years, so little has stayed the same. So how do I feel now, sixteen years after my sepsis?

The truth?

Disability on this scale, with four amputations and a half-reconstructed face, well frankly, it's hard to live through. It's awkward, painful, frustrating, ugly, heartbreaking sometimes. You can't easily keep up appearances, there are violent mood swings to manage, and I've found it very difficult to overcome what is a bottomless chasm of private sadness inside. I have driven to the limb centre a thousand times to try and get arms, hands, feet and legs fixed and I've been on longer, more frequent journeys inside my head, trying to overcome the splintered fear and the jagged sorrow that I truly feel. Dealing with it all has been the challenge of my lifetime and continues to be so.

My inner strength has been tested to the very limit. Some days, I go helter-skelter through a minefield of powerful emotion-explosions. There is anger and fear and frustration and a crushing sense of isolation. Sometimes it feels as if no one could possibly understand the difficulties I go through, that I'm somehow stranded with all my strange issues and nobody can save me. When people or systems or organisations put obstacles in my way, I can panic. On occasion, I've been way past the point where I felt able to keep things together, but I have done that: I will always recover, I will always overcome these feelings. Not because it is easy, but because I want to hold on to my dignity and to my family. Quite simply, the love that I have for them is always strong enough to light my way through the darkness. I will be a great husband, I will be a great Dad – no one and nothing will stop me.

The determination and the light shine incredibly bright, flooding my world. I've not really been able to work, but I have had to work – there's no financial safety net. We live in a quiet, rural part of England, with few job opportunities, and I can't easily travel. But as we ran out of money long ago, I had to take what was on offer. So I work in the local call-centre, on minimum wage, taking orders over the phone and answering emails. In more than twelve years doing this job, my hourly wage has increased by less than £1. On one level, for someone with a good degree from one of the best universities in the country, this is seriously frustrating. But on another, the job has saved me – it gave structure to my life when there was only chaos and it has given me an important network of support. In the office, I feel like I am surrounded by an extended family of friends and supporters, and how much is that worth?

I try not to let on when things are really difficult for me. I have ways of sorting myself out, mentally. I've not had a single minute of professional counselling. I don't say that proudly, because it may well have helped. I've avoided it, although to be honest it's not easily accessible in our part of the country. But I'm impatient to get on with everyday life, and I don't want to get into a long period of self-introspection. Also, I don't have the resources to pay for what would no doubt be an extended process of therapy. Having the family around me helps tremendously – although Grace is away at university, we still have Freddy at home, and we have a strong relationship. I go out of my way to be a useful dad when I can be, offering him lifts and taking him to watch football. Freddy and I have been season ticket holders at Leicester City for the last ten years and we've had many epic days together at home and away games. I make a point of not judging him, and I just try to be as encouraging as I can be. We listen to music together at full volume in the car; we laugh a lot. I never had that kind of relationship with my own dad, so the time I've been able to spend with both Freddy and Grace means everything to me. Plenty of men my age don't have that as a positive in their lives.

Grace is a delight. Her kindnesses charm me. We miss her very much but we are naturally incredibly proud of her – not just of what she has already achieved, but more for the happy, funny, caring and intelligent adult she already is.

And of course, it goes without saying, Nic has saved me.

That statement deserves to be repeated: my wife has saved my life.

Sepsis and its aftermath genuinely destroyed me, but during the last sixteen years or so Nic has single-handedly put me back together as a human being and she has set me back on track.

I owe her my life. Quite simply, I would have died without her.

She was there when I first opened my eyes in hospital, after four months in a coma, smiling at me. She held me in her arms then and she told me who I was. She showed me our new baby son then, and told me that everything would be OK. When all I could see was darkness, she showed me the light. She came to see me every day in Addenbrooke's; she brought me food, she brought me drink. She helped me stagger on my prosthetic legs up the garden path and back to a place of safety, to the home I loved. *Every night, she carried me up the stairs.* She washed me, fed me, dressed me, she put on plasters when I was cut, brought me a million glasses of water, counted out thousands of tablets, drove me to daily appointments over years and years and years. She helped me fill in a billion forms, she encouraged me to start writing again, she gave me the confidence to go and look for a job.

I am so lucky. Quite possibly, the luckiest man in the world. Nic does all these things for me, but that's not why I love her: I love her for herself. For the way she looks, for the way she is, for the easy way we get on with each other. For all her kindness and for her seemingly endless positive energy.

My own resilience is all down to her because she has given me all the world to live for.

The world. I look outwards now, not inwards. Don't get me wrong – some days are still difficult, occasionally very painful. I suffer from powerful post-traumatic stress (PTSD) and my health can be erratic. I feel the pressure of trying to get by on a low income just as badly as many millions of others in the UK. The early years after my amputations were incredibly hard to deal with on so many different levels, but somehow… somehow we have survived. And being involved in making the film, *Starfish*, has been a transformative experience.

The film itself is also a beautiful thing. It stands on its own. It was over ten years in the making, and we collaborated closely with the director Bill Clark in scripting and conceptualisation. Bill is a long-time friend, so we always had confidence that the portrayal of our story would be sensitive, creative and insightful – but the end result exceeded our expectations. The on-screen chemistry between Tom Riley and Joanne Froggatt is precious, compelling, subtle and entirely true to how it was between Nic and me. I treasure the memory of those early years when we lived up by the lake in Hambleton. I was so very happy looking after baby Grace there, so I'm exceptionally touched that the film stands as a record of this. Tom and Jo look so happy and in love with each other in those early scenes, and that is exactly how I remember that period of my life.

I appeared as a body double for actor Tom Riley in a handful of scenes in the movie and this was a fascinating experience. I started my working life as an actor, so it felt natural for me to be on set and to make my contribution. I wasn't out of my depth and I felt a strong, intuitive connection to every scene – I suppose in a way it was vital that I did.

Nic worked throughout the filming in the art

department. There was a fair amount of set building and set dressing – for example, the hospital and operating theatre scenes were filmed in a set she helped build inside a hangar at a local RAF base. She also appears as an extra in one of the scenes, as do Grace and Freddy. We were all proud and excited to be involved. So *Starfish* well and truly is a family affair.

The film has taken us to some great places and we've been introduced to some amazing people. We've been photographed on red carpets, interviewed by national newspapers, appeared on TV sofas, and on the radio. When it's full on, the attention can be dazzling and disorientating, but to be perfectly honest, I like it. I feel at home in that world. Even when the questions are awkward, or intimate, I find a way to respond. Our story is truly incredible and I like to tell it. It all feels like a celebration. That's mostly because at heart, it's so simple. Oh yes, on the medical level, it's about sepsis, and there will be some people who haven't heard about that. But on a deeper level, *Starfish* is just a really powerful love story, and everyone, the whole world over, can relate to that.

The film speaks for me. For Nic and for me, as individuals, as a couple, as parents, as survivors. Now, I feel as if we have a voice.

Every time I go out, I have people coming up to me, and they say one of two things. First, they tell me that I'm an inspiration. Well... In my mind, surviving and overcoming sepsis, as I have done, has been largely out of self-interest: I have a beautiful wife and two amazing children and there was never any question that I would fight like the last warrior on earth to hold on to them. There has never been a moment's doubt about that.

Second, there are some people who tell me that they have a friend or a family member affected by sepsis. It's always hard to respond, especially to the parents of those who have lost children. My heart breaks every time I have to listen to their familiar stories. But I listen carefully, and I always try to remember the name of the son, daughter, grandchild, wife, husband or friend who died. I feel that the names of these people must never be forgotten, so I make a point of saying their names out loud, repeating them in conversation.

In a strange, wonderful way, knowing the names of these people and hearing their stories helps me and gives me strength, because I feel that in some small way I can

speak for them – I can stand up in front of people, I can describe the impact of sepsis, talk about the profound damage, but also spread hope and understanding by telling my own story of resilience and survival.

✳

So that's what I'm doing now. I'm still working in the call centre, but I'm taking every opportunity to speak in public about how sepsis has affected me and to publicise all the good work of the UK Sepsis Trust. I want to demonstrate in public that a person can survive and grow through massive trauma by cultivating strong relationships with allies, by creating strong networks of support, by adjusting goals to reflect realistic targets and by slowing down. I find public speaking very exciting and rewarding, and I am hoping to develop my speaking style even further to help motivate and inspire people to value the good things they have in their lives on a more general level.

The way I see it, everyone goes through change. Mine has been shocking and radical, but everyone faces challenge at some point in their life. To each individual, whether it's a divorce they are going through, a bereavement, an illness, the loss of a job, a relocation, a financial crisis, a separation, or some other kind of sudden setback – well, to every single person going through change, that process can be just as profound, just as crippling as my own. The knock-on effects on their family and friends can be equally severe. We all see this on a daily basis whenever we switch on the news, with shocking sudden accidents, crises and terrorist attacks. Life is unpredictable and the extent to which individuals can maintain control over key aspects of their lives is changing quickly. So I feel I can stand and speak for these people, and talk about how we can be resilient, rising above our challenges, overcoming them.

More than that, I truly believe that by infusing our lives with positivity, kindness and co-operation with one another, we can repair the damage that life does to us along the way, meeting to the challenges we face every day.

By doing this, and *never* giving up, *never* accepting defeat, we become better people, happier individuals, more useful as husbands, wives and partners, more inspiring as parents too.

So, in a way, because I understand this, because I genuinely feel positive about the role I now have to be conciliatory, accepting, creative, friendly and forward-looking, sepsis has been the making of me.

Thank you for reading our book – it means a lot to us.

Please hand it on to someone you care about and ask them to read it too.

Please also keep a note by you of these symptoms of sepsis:

S   Shivering, fever, or very cold
E   Extreme pain, or general discomfort ('worst ever')
P   Pale or discoloured skin
S   Sleepy, difficult to rouse, confused
I   'I feel like I might die'
S   Short of breath

Watch out for a combination of these symptoms – it can often arrive as a complication of another underlying condition, even in hospital. If you do suspect sepsis, be resolute and be quick, call a doctor on an emergency basis, ring 999 or go into a hospital and say the words out loud: 'I suspect sepsis…'

We wish you well with all the challenges you face, now and in the future.

*

Last night, Freddy and I watched Leicester City play in the FA Cup. They scored a last-minute winner, a wonder goal, right in front of us. Just before that, we had dinner in Freddy's favourite restaurant.

Grace is coming home from university this weekend. I'm waiting for Nic now – she should be finishing work in ten minutes or so. I know she'll come back through the front door smiling.

And after everything that's happened, I'll smile back.

SOME FACTS
ABOUT SEPSIS

Thanks to the work of the UK Sepsis Trust (SepsisTrust.org) in collaboration with UK health professionals, a picture is being charted of the scale of the problem and the impact not only on individuals and their families, but NHS budgets and the wider economy.

In a recent report from the University of York it has been proposed that sepsis costs the UK economy between £11.2 and £15.6 billion a year. These costs are borne by families such as ours. It is not that sepsis is becoming more common, but improved reporting and awareness amongst the public and health professionals is bringing better, more accurate data.

We calculated that Tom's sepsis in December 1999 has cost us personally and the NHS £1.4 million. By the time we reach retirement age this will have risen to a cool £2 million, excluding benefits. It is not difficult to understand the £15 billion tally, given that in the UK alone, last year up to 260,000 people may have developed the condition.

> *Early symptoms can include fever, low body temperature, chills, shivering, raised heartbeat and rapid breathing. Symptoms of sepsis or septic shock may develop soon after including feeling dizzy or faint, a change in mental state, diarrhoea, nausea and vomiting, slurred speech, severe muscle pain, severe breathlessness, reduced urine production, cold, clammy and pale or mottled skin and loss of consciousness.*

Unlike many other potentially fatal diseases we are not looking for a cure or complex treatment: sepsis is easily treated with antibiotics and a simple, well-documented set of steps that can be administered in A&E. The key is awareness, by us, the community and by the healthcare professionals we encounter when we first start to feel unwell.

None of the events in this book should have happened, but they did. No other family deserves to go through this, but they will. Every person you tell, every post, every blog or message or tweet, every conversation at work, down the coffee shop, or over the dinner table, will diminish those numbers.

Let's save some lives.

Thank you for reading, and more importantly, thank you for *sharing*.

Nic Ray

4 March 2017

APPENDICES

Below is the hospital's official chronology of events.

10 12 99 P. vomiting for 10 hours with
temperature. Asleep now. Domperidone.

7.10pm – V. urgent call from partner. Has had
diarrhoea – seen this morning by Dr Young and
given Domperidone. Took at lunchtime, vomited
immediately after. Took again and a few hours later
wife found him, lips blue, cold peripheries, swollen
blotchy face. On arrival responsive, oriented but
drowsy – blue lips, peripheral shutdown. Chest,
no wheeze, clear. Pulse 120 regular BP 90/60.
Impression: anaphylactic shock. 02 put on by

mask, given IM 1:10,000 1ML Adrenaline IV
access – 10mg Piriton 100mg hydrocortisone.
Ambulance arrived approximately 7.25pm – taken
to Peterborough A&E.

8.29pm A & E Records. History of being unwell
for last 18 hours with nausea and vomiting. Took
Domperidone and since then has developed rash,
SOB, cold extremities. Rash on trunk on face.
Tachypnoea, tachycardia, hypotensive.

Patient became unwell approximately 0300 this
morning. Nausea, vomiting – vomited x 4 since
1400 hours. Given Domperidone by GP. Now
unwell as above, SOB, pale, cold extremities,
tachypnoea. Observations: pulse 136 resps 34
BP 88/71 temp 37 SaO2 83% BM 2.6. Casualty
officer Choudhry 20.30. Referred to Medicine
21.30. Diagnosis: anaphylactic shock.

10.30pm – reviewed in A&E. History from wife:
vomiting since ++3am today. Had sausages for
dinner at 8pm the previous night – ? – poorly
cooked. Vomiting persisted throughout the day.
Domperidone prescribed by GP. Had 3 tabs at
2pm, had 2 tabs at 5pm. Developed skin rash after
second dose initially over anterior chest wall –

spread over the face and trunk with facial swelling.
No pruritus. No difficulty in breathing or wheeze.
No known allergies. Normally fit and well. PMH:
nil of note. Non-smoker, alcohol, approximately
1 bottle of wine per week. On examination looks
very ill. Red, blotchy rash mainly over the face
and trunk. Not breathless at rest, apyrexial. Pulse
130 regular BP 121/75 (88/71 on admission).
CNS – alert, oriented, GCS 15/15. Impression:
anaphylactic reaction, probably to Domperidone.
Platelets 40 and dropping. Crt 256 urea 11.1
CRP<10. ECG sinus (illegible) approximately 140.
Blood culture. ABG's on 100 O2 21.16 hours. Plt
7.26 pCO2 4.3 pO2 58.8 BC 15 BE 11 – metabolic
acidosis. Plan: IV hydrocortisone 1009 mg qds,
Chlorphenamine 4mg 6-hourly, observe closely
– vital signs half-hourly. Repeat blood gases and
FBC, CXR – portable prominent right hilum and
bronchovascular pattern. Signed (illegible) SPR.

00.30 am – admitted with anaphylactic reaction ?
to Domperidone requiring IM and IV adrenaline.
Normal eosinophil count. Note: renal impairment
– Cr 256 Ur 11.1 Acidotic. Thrombocytopenia.
Lymphopenia. No clotting available. Generally
feeling well in self today. No wheeze/stridor/
tongue swelling. No past history of medical

problems. On examination two-week history of cold. Denies any diarrhoea. Temp 37.6 pulse 120. CNS: tone left = right = flaccid. Sensation: grossly intact for soft touch. Impression: (1) anaphylactic shock ? precipitant (2) HUS/TTP, Guillain-Barré – renal impairment and falling platelets with areflexia. Plan: (1) close monitoring TPR/BP 15 mins (2) repeat FBC U&E's clotting ESR CRP ABG's LFT's TAT (3) catheterise (4) fluid balance IV fluids (5) stool – M, C&S. CXR – NAD. ECG: sinus tachycardia, not acute/ischaemic changes. Remains very ill, coagulation screen (verbal report) APTT > 100 PT 64 DDIMER increasing fast. Diagnosis: disseminated intravascular coagulation. Plan: needs anaesthetic review with a view to transfer to ITU.

01.00 am – patient drowsy but fully oriented. Very poor sensation to legs and peripheries cold. Rash – purple all over body, worse to face. Eyes bloodshot and tongue white. Doctor informed re poor sensation. Reviewed patient. Feeling breathless on exertion. 02 at 101 sats only 83% doctor informed. Has been given adrenaline, hydrocortisone and Gelofusine. BP stable on warding but patient remains very tachycardic – doctor aware. 01.30 sats 93%.

03.10 catheter in situ, to be recorded hourly.

05.00 – BP remains low. Very concerned re patient's condition. Duty Manager contacted. Reviewed by Anaesthetist – for ITU.

05.24 hours – admitted to ITU from IZ. Quite unresponsive, very low saturations and BP. Immediately intubated and NG tube passed. Started on haemofiltration. Blood gases taken pO2 50 therefore 02 down to 60% Ph 7. Doctors aware urgent blood taken. Blood cultures taken. Benzylpenicillin given 2.4g.

Wife spoken to by Consultant Anaesthetist. Explained that diagnosis was now thought to be septicaemia or blood poisoning rather than food poisoning or anaphylaxis. Severity of condition highlighted. Informed that we are still unaware of a definite diagnosis but feel this is a meningococcal septicaemia. The treatment he is receiving covers all possibilities.

Plastic surgeon notes. Nose: necrotic distal ½ to ¾ – full thickness cartilage probably non-viable. Lips: full thickness loss – mummified. Cheeks: full thickness loss – mummified. Scalp and neck clear. Trunk potentially clear, anteriorly area of deep dermal necrosis and FT losses – patchy. Upper limbs: forearms blistering and fixed staining and deep dermal necrosis. Dry gangrene of all fingertips and thumb tips right > left different levels. Lower limbs soft on pressure. Legs and calves deep dermal to FT skin loss. Toes: right little toe mummified. Penis – mummified skin prepuce. Ears surprisingly largely spared: small area. Summary: previously fit with multiple-digit gangrene. Large areas dead skin especially on the forearms and calves and lower face. Plan: bactigras dressings to forearms, calves and other blistered areas once a day. Polyfax or Chloromycetin ointment to lips, nose, tip of penis tds. Foot drop splints – minimum at night. Short term: once he is medically better approximately 10–14 days (1) debridement of all mummified digits and lower face (2) excision of the dead skin and split skin grafting in stages.

He is likely to be in hospital for approximately 2 months for plastic surgery alone. Long-term revisions as required. Discussed with family, wife, sister and mother – explained that he will need amputation of all limbs.

Poor prognosis emphasised and informed wife that he may die.

ACKNOWLEDGEMENTS

To my sister Nina, for all the miles you drove, for your laughter, for your love.

To my late mother, Angela – you fought so hard to make me what I am, I never forget that.

To Adam, taken from us too soon. Love you forever, brother. You taught me how to be.

To our daughter Grace – for being kind, fun, and for eating those dinners I cooked you.

To Freddy, my son, my friend. So proud of you. How brilliant has it been at the football?

To Jean, my mother-in-law, who somehow held us all together through these years.

To Nic, my wife. When I had no hope, you came and saved me. I owe you everything.

To Suzanne, who looked after the children in the early years of crisis with kindness and stability. To Sal, Nic's best friend, such a great voice on the phone – thank you for being there; Sarah and Tony – you gave us unconditional love and friendship, and kept us grounded; Nia and Tony, for tea, biscuits and help with finding all the right words; Jim Shields, a creative dynamo and an absolute rock of a friend through half a lifetime; Neil Davenport, for your music, for showing us how to live, and fixing things; Shona Stapleton, who helped with practical stuff and kept our chaos organised; David Househam, for making us laugh when days were hard. That was so important.

To all the medical people who have helped me, doctors, nurses, NHS auxiliaries, especially the hospital cleaners and porters; Steve Young, GP, you were a good friend to us; Mr Charles Malata, you helped to reconstruct me; Mr Terreblanche, you literally saved my life.

To all my friends at the UK Sepsis Trust, especially Ron

ACKNOWLEDGEMENTS

Daniels and Sarah Hamilton-Fairley. To Pippa Bagnall, who has helped us to develop as public speakers with Resilience+Co. To our friends in the Sepsis Community, living and not, especially Melissa and Paul Mead and their beautiful boys Arthur and William.
To Sonia Adrissi, Terence Canning, Manuela Sforza and Sue and Sam Morrish, and all their families.

To Bill Clark, writer and film director at Origami Films. Bill, Starfish speaks for us and all those affected by Sepsis in such a unique, beautiful and creative way. It means a lot to us that you cared so much; Pippa Cross, Goose Charlton, CrossDay Productions, Mel Paton, Ros and John Hubbard; Jo Froggatt and Tom Riley – you did us proud; the kids who played the kids – Ellie Copping, Oli Cunliffe, Joe McErlean, Isla Crowther, Alex Sedgwick and Elsie Adams – you are family now.

To the Hudson family, legendary, stalwart, unblinking. We never felt like we were on our own, and that was a good thing.

To LandsEnd UK, for giving Tom a way back into work, and particularly Mark Harris, for your encouragement.

Finally, Liz and Ciara from John Blake Publishing and our literary agent Andrew Lownie.

THE TRUE STORY OF A COUPLE WHOSE LOVE IS TESTED TO ITS LIMIT
AFTER THEIR PERFECT LIFE FALLS APART IN A SINGLE MOMENT

'POWERFULLY MOVING'
Charles Gant - Screen International

'A VERY THOUGHTFUL AND TENDER EXAMINATION OF A
RELATIONSHIP THAT IS TESTED TO THE ABSOLUTE LIMIT'
The Sun